Unusual
Baby Names

Crombie Jardine

PUBLISHING LIMITED
Office 2
3 Edgar Buildings
George Street
Bath
BA1 2FJ

www.crombiejardine.com

This edition first published by
Crombie Jardine Publishing Limited in 2010

Written by Stewart Ferris

ISBN 978-1-906051-38-9

Printed and bound in the UK

Contents

"Any child can tell you that the sole purpose of a middle name is so he can tell when he's really in trouble."

Dennis Frakes

Introduction

IF you want to give someone a name that will stand out for life, look no further than this book. Each of these names has been carefully researched and selected for its originality, rarity, beauty, poetry, meaning, symbolism, humour, or for its downright weirdness. Growing up with one of the names in this book will not be run-of-the-mill. Carrying an unusual name is like having a head start towards celebrity, a label that identifies a person as being special.

Why bother to give a name that is so common that it has to be shared amongst whole swathes of the population when you could choose a name that is so rare that it seems to be reserved for one person alone? How many times have you met someone called 'Golden', or 'Otis', or 'Marmaduke'? Some celebrities don't need to be referred to by both names: when their first name is sufficient for everyone to know who it is, that's the sign of an unusual name. Ringo doesn't need 'Starr'. Elvis didn't need 'Presley'.

Remember that the name given to a child determines their identity for life. It also determines how other people will perceive them. Names have connotations and associations that force preconceptions upon their innocent bearers.

Parents usually take care to avoid names that have obvious bullying or teasing potential (celebrities are the exception to this rule), and that is why potential nicknames are listed with each name in this book. But it's vital to remember that the inventiveness, creativity and sheer ability of children to tease their friends in the playground knows no bounds.

A name that is entirely innocuous at birth, with no known teasing potential whatsoever, can become a source of ridicule a few years down the line due to the arrival of a notoriously dumb sitcom or film character with that name. Even advertising campaigns can change the perception of a name: imagine being called 'Humphrey' in Britain during the 1970s Unigate milk promotion ('Watch out, watch out, there's a Humphrey about').

In deciding what constitutes an 'unusual' name (in the context of English-speaking countries), it would have been easy simply to raid the phone books of exotic lands and fill this tome with Chinese, African and Inuit names. Whilst there are inevitably many names that are of foreign origin in this collection, what I have attempted to do is to restrict the listings to those names which have some degree of familiarity due to their relevance to the culture and history of English-speaking lands.

INTRODUCTION

There are many wonderful names that are familiar to us from the works of Shakespeare yet which rarely see the light of day in the modern world. There are historic people – from the Romans to the Victorians – whose names trip off the tongue in a delightful way when rediscovered. There are Biblical names that are wonderfully evocative and poetic. Additionally, there is a new category of unusual names spawned by celebrities who seem to have a knack for finding (or coining) bizarre and interesting names for their children.

'Unusual' in this book therefore doesn't exclusively mean names you won't have heard before. The hope is that most of the names are ones that are rarely encountered in daily life and which will trigger a pleasant reminder of something long forgotten.

Unusual Names
for Boys

Abraham

Origin and meaning

Hebrew origin, meaning 'father of many nations'.
The descendants of the Biblical Abraham are said to
include both the Arab and the Israeli nations.
Abraham Lincoln, President, and Abraham Simpson,
cartoon character, are the best known American
examples of the name.

Potential nickname alert

Abe, Ham, Hamster.

Adolf

Origin and meaning

German origin, meaning 'noble wolf'.
The name is now tainted by its association with
Hitler, making it an extremely unusual name for
anyone born since 1945.

Potential nickname alert

Führer, Hitler, One-ball.

Agamemnon

Origin and meaning

Greek origin, meaning 'resolute'.
In Greek mythology Agamemnon is a hero, and
appears as a character in Shakespeare's *Troilus and
Cressida*.

Potential nickname alert

Aggie.

Aladdin

Origin and meaning
Arabic origin, meaning 'nobility of faith'.
Aladdin is one of the ancient stories told in the
collection known as *The Arabian Nights*, and is now
best known as a Disney animated film and a popular
pantomime theme.
Potential nickname alert
Al, Laddie.

Alonso

Origin and meaning
German origin, meaning 'noble and ready for war'.
The name is associated with a character from
Shakespeare's *The Tempest*.
Potential nickname alert
Al, Lonny.

Aloysius

Origin and meaning
German origin, meaning 'famous soldier'.
Also the name of a teddy bear that features in Evelyn
Waugh's 1945 novel *Brideshead Revisited*.
Potential nickname alert
Louis, Delicious.

Alvin

Origin and meaning
Old English origin, meaning 'friend of elves'.
Other than Alvin Stardust, the name is best
remembered for its association with animated
chipmunks.
Potential nickname alert
Al, Vino, Vinny, Chipmunk.

Apollo

Origin and meaning
Greek origin, referring to the Greek and Roman god
of music, medicine and enlightenment.
The Apollo space programme succeeded in landing
twelve men on the moon and bringing them safely
home.
Potential nickname alert
Polo, Pillow.

Aramis

Origin and meaning
French origin, first coined by Alexandre Dumas in his
novel *The Three Musketeers* as the name of one of the
protagonists in that book.
Also the name of a brand of fragrance.
Potential nickname alert
Miss, Ari.

Archibald

Origin and meaning
German/French origin, meaning 'faithful' or 'brave'.
The actor Archibald Alexander Leach is better known
by his stage name, Cary Grant.

Potential nickname alert
Archie, Baldy.

Aristotle

Origin and meaning
Greek origin, meaning 'best of all'.
Aristotle was a philosopher in ancient Greece, and
Aristotle Onassis was a 20th-century shipping
magnate who married the widow of John F.
Kennedy.

Potential nickname alert
Ari, Totty, Tootle.

Aston

Origin and meaning
Old English origin, meaning 'town in the east'.
The name is associated with a football team when
combined with Villa and with a luxury sports car
brand when combined with Martin.

Potential nickname alert
Villa, DB5.

Atticus

Origin and meaning

Latin origin, meaning 'from Athens'.

A common ancient Greek name, it was also given to the wise Atticus Finch character in Harper Lee's novel *To Kill a Mockingbird*.

Potential nickname alert

Attic, Lofty.

Attila

Origin and meaning

Hungarian origin, meaning 'father-like', but with overtones of cruelty and viciousness due to its association with the 5th-century German king Attila the Hun.

Potential nickname alert

Hun, Atty.

Audio Science

Origin and meaning

Name coined by US actress and star of *A Knight's Tale* Shannyn Sossamon for her baby boy, born in 2003.

Potential nickname alert

Oddie, Hi Fi.

Augustus

Origin and meaning

Latin origin, meaning 'revered'.

Augustus was an honorary name given to Roman emperors, and Augustus Gloop is a character in Roald Dahl's novel and the film *Charlie and the Chocolate Factory*.

Potential nickname alert

Gus, Gusto, Gloop.

Balthazar

Origin and meaning

Phoenician origin, meaning 'God protects the King'.

The name was liked so much by Shakespeare that he used it in his plays *Romeo and Juliet*, *The Merchant of Venice*, *Much Ado About Nothing* and *The Comedy of Errors*.

Potential nickname alert

Bizarre, Zar.

Bamber

Origin and meaning

English origin, relating to the location of Bamber Bridge in northern England.

Best known for the television presenter and *University Challenge* host Bamber Gascoigne.

Potential nickname alert

Bambi, Baz.

Bartholomew

Origin and meaning
Hebrew origin, meaning 'son of ploughed land'.
The Biblical Bartholomew was one of the twelve
Apostles of Jesus, and Bartholomew Simpson is a
cartoon character better known as 'Bart'.
Potential nickname alert
Bart.

Basil

Origin and meaning
Greek origin, meaning 'royal', also said to have Arabic
origin meaning 'brave'.
As well as being a popular herb, it's the name given by
John Cleese to his hotel manager character in the
sitcom *Fawlty Towers*.
Potential nickname alert
Baz, Fawlty.

Benvolio

Origin and meaning
Italian origin, meaning 'kindly' or 'benevolent'.
Used by Shakespeare as the name of Romeo's cousin
in *Romeo and Juliet*.
Potential nickname alert
Ben, Benny.

Blanket

Origin and meaning
Nickname given by Michael Jackson to one of his sons, Prince Michael Jackson II.
Jackson equated the name 'Blanket' to a blessing and considered it a sign of love and affection.

Potential nickname alert
Blanky, Wacko.

Boris

Origin and meaning
Russian origin, meaning 'glory in battle'.
Boris Yeltsin was the first President of democratic Russia, Boris Becker was the youngest Wimbledon winner in 1985, and Boris Johnson became Mayor of London in 2008.

Potential nickname alert
Bozzer, Bozo, Doris.

Branson

Origin and meaning
German origin, meaning 'sword'.
Branson Roberts is a fictional character in a series of science fiction novels by American author Kevin J. Anderson.

Potential nickname alert
Branston, Virgin.

Brooklyn

Origin and meaning
Dutch origin, meaning either 'broken land' or 'land by the brook'.
Once best known as a New York borough, Victoria and David Beckham have since usurped the name for their son.
Potential nickname alert
Spice Boy, Bridge, Manhattan.

Buzz

Origin and meaning
Originating in recent times as a nickname, it has become accepted as a boy's name due to the popularity of astronaut Buzz Aldrin who was the lunar module pilot on the first moon landing.
The cartoon character Buzz Lightyear has further enhanced the coolness of this name.
Potential nickname alert
Buzzy Bee.

Caesar

Origin and meaning
Latin origin, meaning 'head of hair'.
Julius Caesar was a dictator who helped to form the Roman Empire, and a Caesar salad is a dish made from lettuce, croutons, olive oil and parmesan cheese.
Potential nickname alert
Julius, Kaiser.

Carlisle

Origin and meaning
Old English origin, meaning 'castle of Luel', referring to the fortified town founded by the Romans in northern England.
Carlisle Floyd is an American opera composer.
Potential nickname alert
Carl.

Caroll

Origin and meaning
German and Gaelic origin, meaning 'manly' or 'strong fighter'.
Despite its macho meanings the name is more commonly associated with the girl's version (with a single 'l'). Caroll Spinney is an American puppeteer who worked on *Sesame Street*.
Potential nickname alert
Carl, Carry.

Cash

Origin and meaning
Latin origin, an abbreviation of 'Cassius'. Also means 'money' in English.
Cash Asmussen is an American jockey who won more than 3,000 races in his career.
Potential nickname alert
Money, Dosh, Cashew.

Caspar

Origin and meaning
Persian origin, meaning 'treasurer' and said to be the
name of one of the Three Wise Men who travelled to
see the baby Jesus.
Claudia Schiffer's son is called Caspar, not to be
confused with the friendly ghost character, which is
spelt 'Casper'.
Potential nickname alert
Caspy, Ghost.

Cassius

Origin and meaning
Latin origin, meaning 'empty' or 'poor'.
Caius Cassius is a major character in the Shakespeare
play *Julius Caesar*, and Cassius Clay was the birth
name of boxer Mohammed Ali.
Potential nickname alert
Cash, Clay.

Cedric

Origin and meaning
Welsh origin, meaning 'a great prize'.
Sir Walter Scott first coined the modern usage of the
name in his novel *Ivanhoe*, and Cedric Price was a
British architect.
Potential nickname alert
Ced, Rick, Cheddar.

Chad

Origin and meaning
Old English origin, meaning 'warlike'.
Also refers to a country in Central Africa as well as a popular graffiti drawing that originated during World War II showing someone with a long nose peering over a wall and complaining about shortages of food and other war-restricted things.
Potential nickname alert
Chadwick, Chaddie.

Chadwick

Origin and meaning
Old English origin, meaning 'dairy farm belonging to Caedda'.
Chadwick Tyler is a New York photographer, and Chadwick Trujillo is an American astronomer.
Potential nickname alert
Chad, Cheddar.

Chaucer

Origin and meaning
French origin, meaning 'shoe maker'.
Geoffrey Chaucer was a 14th-century poet famous for writing *The Canterbury Tales*, and is considered the 'father' of English literature. Chaucer Elliot was a Canadian sportsman who died in 1913.
Potential nickname alert
Chaucy, Chalky.

Chevy

Origin and meaning
French origin, short for 'Chevalier', meaning 'knight' or 'horseman', but now carries less glamorous overtones of American cars.
Chevy Chase is an American comedian and film star.
Potential nickname alert
Chewy.

Claudius

Origin and meaning
Latin origin, meaning 'lame'.
Claudius is Hamlet's unpleasant uncle in Shakespeare's tragedy, and was also a Roman emperor as fictionalised in the novel and television series *I, Claudius*.
Potential nickname alert
Clod, Cloudy.

Clement

Origin and meaning
Latin origin, meaning 'merciful'.
Clement Attlee was the British Prime Minister following World War II, and Clement Freud was a writer, politician, chef and BBC Radio 4 game show regular.
Potential nickname alert
Clem, Cement, Clementine, Clemmy.

Cliff

Origin and meaning
Old English origin, a variant of 'Clifford' meaning 'ford by a cliff'.
Cliff Richard is a record-breaking pop star with number one hits in five consecutive decades, and Cliff Michelmore was a BBC television presenter during four consecutive decades.
Potential nickname alert
Cliffy, Clit, Whiffy.

Clint

Origin and meaning
English origin, a variant of 'Clinton' meaning 'fenced settlement'.
Clint Eastwood is an American actor famous for playing film roles of tough characters in the 1960s and 1970s.
Potential nickname alert
Eastwood, Clit.

Conrad

Origin and meaning
German origin, meaning 'wise adviser'.
The name is a familiar fixture on the list of German kings, and is also known for Monty Python's animated sketch 'Conrad Poohs and his Dancing Teeth'.
Potential nickname alert
Con, Connie.

Constantine

Origin and meaning

Latin origin, meaning 'steadfast'.

Constantine I was a Roman emperor who achieved the transformation of the Roman Empire from polytheism to Christianity. Susannah Constantine is a television presenter who achieved the transformation of plain women into slightly less plain women.

Potential nickname alert

Con, Connie, Constant, Constipation.

Corbin

Origin and meaning

French origin, meaning 'dark hair'.

The American actor Corbin Bleu starred in Disney's film series *High School Musical*.

Potential nickname alert

Cor, Corby, Dustbin.

Cornelius

Origin and meaning

Latin origin, meaning 'horn'.

Dr. Cornelius is an ape character played by British actor Roddy McDowall in the 1968 version of the film *Planet of the Apes*, and Cornelius Chase is the real name of American actor Chevy Chase.

Potential nickname alert

Corny, Nelly.

Cyril

Origin and meaning
Greek origin, meaning 'Lord'.
Cyril Smith was a Liberal Democrat M.P. famous for
his rotundity, and Cyril Fletcher was a comedian who
appeared regularly on the television show *That's Life*.
Potential nickname alert
Squirrel, Cereal.

Dartagnan

Origin and meaning
French origin, meaning 'from Artagnan', sometimes
spelt 'd'Artagnan'.
D'Artagnan is a character in the novel *The Three
Musketeers* by Alexandre Dumas.
Potential nickname alert
Dart, Dartonion, Arty.

Demetrius

Origin and meaning
Greek origin, meaning 'goddess of the harvest'.
Demetrius is one of the young lovers in Shakespeare's
A Midsummer Night's Dream.
Potential nickname alert
Dee, Demi.

Digby

Origin and meaning
Norse origin, meaning 'settlement near a ditch'.
Best known for *Digby: The Biggest Dog in the World*,
the 1973 film starring Jim Dale and Spike Milligan,
and Digby Jones is a British businessman and life peer.
Potential nickname alert
Digger.

Dupre

Origin and meaning
French origin, meaning 'from the meadow', also spelt
'Dupree'.
Owen Wilson played Randolph Dupree in the 2006
film *You, Me and Dupree*.
Potential nickname alert
Dupe, Dupo.

Ebenezer

Origin and meaning
Hebrew origin, meaning 'stone of the help'.
The name is usually associated with meanness
following Charles Dickens' choice of this first name
for his miser character Scrooge in the novel *A
Christmas Carol*.
Potential nickname alert
Scrooge, Ben, E.

Elijah

Origin and meaning
Hebrew origin, meaning 'God is my Lord'.
The name has become famous following the actor
Elijah Wood's starring role in *The Lord of the Rings*
films.
Potential nickname alert
Eli, Elly.

Elvis

Origin and meaning
English origin, meaning 'all wise'.
Saint Elvis of Munster was a 5th-century Irish
bishop, and Elvis Presley was the undisputed King
of Rock 'n' Roll.
Potential nickname alert
Elly, The King.

Emmett

Origin and meaning
German origin, meaning 'universal'.
Dr. Emmett Brown is the eccentric inventor
character in the film trilogy *Back to the Future* in
which he creates a time machine out of a
DeLorean sports car.
Potential nickname alert
Em, Emmy.

Engelbert

Origin and meaning
German origin, meaning 'shining Angle', referring to the Germanic race known as the Angles.
Engelbert Humperdinck (born Arnold George Dorsey) is a British singer and pianist who chose to name himself after a German opera composer.
Potential nickname alert
Bert, Bertie, Gilbert.

Errol

Origin and meaning
Old English origin, meaning 'Earl' or 'nobleman'.
Errol Flynn was an Australian-born actor famous for his swashbuckling roles in the 1930s and 1940s.
Potential nickname alert
Earl.

Ethan

Origin and meaning
Hebrew origin, meaning 'strong'.
Ethan Hawke is an American film actor who appeared alongside River Phoenix in the 1985 film *Explorers* and also featured in *Dead Poets Society*.
Potential nickname alert
Ethanol, Nathan.

Eugene

Origin and meaning
Greek origin, meaning 'noble'.
Eugene ('Gene') Roddenberry created the television
series *Star Trek*, Eugene ('Gene') Kranz was the NASA
Flight Director who oversaw the landing of the first
men on the moon, and astronaut Eugene Cernan was
the last person to walk on the moon.
Potential nickname alert
Gene.

Fabien

Origin and meaning
Latin origin, a variant of 'Fabian' meaning 'bean
grower'.
Fabien Barthez was a Manchester United goalkeeper
who helped the French national team win the World
Cup in 1998.
Potential nickname alert
Fab.

Felix

Origin and meaning
Latin origin, meaning 'happy' or 'fortunate'.
The name has strong feline connotations due to the
Felix the Cat cartoons from the 1920s and a brand of
cat food.
Potential nickname alert
Felix the Cat, Flix.

Ferris

Origin and meaning
Gaelic origin, meaning 'iron worker'.
Ferris Bueller is the lead character in the iconic 1980s
American film *Ferris Bueller's Day Off*, and the Ferris
Wheel fairground attraction was invented in 1893 in
Chicago.
Potential nickname alert
Bueller, Wheel.

Finial

Origin and meaning
English origin, meaning 'final', relating to the last
piece of ornament to be fitted to a roof or piece of
furniture.
Potential nickname alert
Finny, Fin.

Florian

Origin and meaning
Latin origin, meaning 'flower'.
Florian Hugo is a world-renowned chef working in
New York, and is also a descendant of the great
French writer Victor Hugo.
Potential nickname alert
Flo, Flora.

Fortescue

Origin and meaning
French origin, meaning 'strong shield'.
Fortescue Flannery was a Conservative M.P. for
Maldon from 1910 to 1922, and the Fortescue River
runs through Western Australia.
Potential nickname alert
Forty, Tessa.

Fortinbras

Origin and meaning
English origin, created as a name for a Norwegian
crown prince character in Shakespeare's play *Hamlet*.
The name has appeared more recently as a character
in the Japanese video game *Onimusha: Warlords*.
Potential nickname alert
Forty, Tin-bra.

Franklin

Origin and meaning
English origin, meaning 'free man or landowner'.
Franklin D. Roosevelt was the only President of the
United States to have been elected to office four
times, dying early into his fourth term shortly before
the end of World War II.
Potential nickname alert
Frankie.

Gaelan

Origin and meaning
Greek origin, meaning 'calm'.
Gaelan Connell is an American actor who appeared in
the 2000 film *Chocolat* and took the lead role in the
2009 film *Bandslam*.
Potential nickname alert
Gay, Gail.

Galahad

Origin and meaning
Welsh origin, referring to the knight of King Arthur's
Round Table, Sir Galahad, who was renowned for his
purity and chastity.
Galahad Threepwood is a fictional character created
by the British author P.G. Wodehouse for his
Blandings novels.
Potential nickname alert
Gal, Gala.

Ganymede

Origin and meaning
Greek origin, referring to the mythical Greek prince
who was said to have been abducted by the god Zeus.
Also the name of one of Jupiter's moons.
Potential nickname alert
Gange, Ganner.

Geronimo

Origin and meaning
Greek origin, meaning 'sacred'.
Geronimo was a Native American Apache who became famous in the late 19th and early 20th century, and Geronimo James is the son of Alex James from the British band Blur.
Potential nickname alert
Jerome, Jerry, Nemo.

Giuseppe

Origin and meaning
Hebrew origin, a form of 'Joseph' meaning 'God will increase it'.
A Sloppy Giuseppe is a type of pizza offered by the restaurant chain Pizza Express, and Giuseppe Verdi was a 19th-century Italian composer.
Potential nickname alert
Sloppy, Gypsie.

Goliath

Origin and meaning
Hebrew origin, meaning 'huge and powerful'.
In the Old Testament the giant Goliath was a warrior who was slain with a slingshot to the head by the diminutive David.
Potential nickname alert
Golly.

Gus

Origin and meaning

Latin origin, an abbreviation of 'Augustus' meaning 'revered'.

Gus Grissom was the second American to fly in space, and Gus Hedges is a character in the British sitcom *Drop the Dead Donkey*.

Potential nickname alert

Gust, Goose.

Hadrian

Origin and meaning

Latin origin, meaning 'from Hadria'.

The Roman Emperor Hadrian is remembered for the wall he built to separate England from Scotland.

Potential nickname alert

Hades, Wall.

Hamlet

Origin and meaning

Anglicised form of the Danish name 'Amleth'.

Hamlet is the troubled Danish prince with a penchant for soliloquy in Shakespeare's eponymous tragedy.

Potential nickname alert

Ham, Hammy, Toby (To be or not to be), Omelette.

Hannibal

Origin and meaning
Phoenician origin, meaning 'the glory of God'.
Hannibal was a Carthaginian soldier famous for
crossing the Alps with elephants around 200 BC, and
Hannibal Lecter is a fictional cannibal and serial killer
who features in a series of novels and films.
Potential nickname alert
Han, Honey, Honeyball.

Hartley

Origin and meaning
Old English origin, meaning 'stag wood'.
Hartley Hare was the moth-eaten star of the 1970s
children's television show *Pipkins*, and J.R. Hartley
was a fictional character from a Yellow Pages
television advert in the 1980s.
Potential nickname alert
Hart, Smarty.

Heathcliff

Origin and meaning
English origin, meaning 'a heath on a cliff'.
Heathcliff is a character from Emily Brontë's novel
Wuthering Heights. He also features in Kate Bush's
song of the same title.
Potential nickname alert
Heath, Cliff, Cliffy.

Hector

Origin and meaning
Greek origin, meaning 'steadfast'.
The French composer Berlioz proudly bore this
name, as does a character in *A Series of Unfortunate
Events*, the series of children's novels by Lemony
Snicket.
Potential nickname alert
Heck.

Heinz

Origin and meaning
German origin, meaning 'home ruler'.
Professor Heinz Wolff is a German-born scientist and
television presenter, best known for the series *The
Great Egg Race*.
Potential nickname alert
Heiny, Ketchup.

Herbert

Origin and meaning
German origin, meaning 'bright host'.
Herbert Hoover became the 31st President of the
United States in 1929, and Herbert Austin founded
the Austin Motor Company in 1905.
Potential nickname alert
Herbie, Herb, Bertie.

Homer

Origin and meaning
Greek origin, meaning 'pledge'.
Homer was an ancient Greek writer famous for his epic poems *Odyssey* and *Iliad*, and Homer Simpson is the doughnut-loving father character in the cartoon series *The Simpsons*.
Potential nickname alert
Homy, Simpson.

Horatio

Origin and meaning
Latin origin, meaning 'time'.
Horatio Caine is a fictional detective character in the American television series *CSI: Miami*, Horatio Hornblower is a fictional naval character in the novels of C.S. Forester, and Horatio Nelson was Britain's greatest naval hero.
Potential nickname alert
Horace, Ratio.

Hortensius

Origin and meaning
Latin origin, meaning 'garden'.
Quintus Hortensius was appointed dictator of Rome in 287 BC, and Hortensius is also the name of a crater on the moon.
Potential nickname alert
Horty, Horten.

Humphrey

Origin and meaning
German origin, meaning 'peaceful warrior'.
Humphrey Bogart was an American actor famous for
films such as *Casablanca*, and Humphrey Lyttelton
was a jazz musician and former chairman of the BBC
Radio 4 programme *I'm Sorry I Haven't a Clue*.
Potential nickname alert
Humph, Hump, Humpty Dumpty.

Icarus

Origin and meaning
Greek origin, referring to the son of Daedalus who in
Greek mythology attached feathers to his body with
wax, then flew so close to the sun that the wax
melted causing him to crash to his death.
Potential nickname alert
Ike, Iccy.

Ichabod

Origin and meaning
Hebrew origin, meaning 'inglorious'.
Ichabod Crane is a character in the Washington Irving
short story *The Legend of Sleepy Hollow* which has been
made into many film adaptations.
Potential nickname alert
Itchy, Icky, Bod.

Ignatius

Origin and meaning
Latin origin, meaning 'fiery'.
This name was given to Cate Blanchett's third son, and Sir Arthur Ignatius Conan Doyle was the author of the books about Sherlock Holmes.
Potential nickname alert
Iggy, Nato, Igneous.

Jagger

Origin and meaning
Old English origin, meaning 'peddler'.
Jagger Cates is a fictional character from the American television series *General Hospital*, and Jagger Chase is an American actor.
Potential nickname alert
Jago, Jag, Jaggers.

Jared

Origin and meaning
Hebrew origin, meaning 'descent'.
Jared Harris is an English actor who has appeared in films such as *The Curious Case of Benjamin Button*, *Oceans Twelve* and *Shadow Magic*.
Potential nickname alert
Jay, Jar, Jarhead.

Jarvis

Origin and meaning
German origin, meaning 'spear servant'.
Jarvis Cocker is the former lead singer of the British
pop band Pulp, and Jarvis Lorry is a character in the
novel *A Tale of Two Cities* by Charles Dickens.
Potential nickname alert
Jay, Jarface.

Jasper

Origin and meaning
Greek origin, meaning 'speckled stone'.
Jasper Carrott OBE is a British comedian, Jasper
Beardly is a minor character in the American cartoon
show *The Simpsons*, and Jasper Conran OBE is a
British fashion designer.
Potential nickname alert
Jazz, Jasp, Casper.

Jermaine

Origin and meaning
Latin origin, meaning 'brother'.
Jermaine Jackson was the original lead singer of The
Jackson Five before his younger brother Michael took
over in 1968.
Potential nickname alert
German, Germs, Jeremy.

Jermajesty

Origin and meaning
Name given to one of Jermaine Jackson's sons for reasons that are best known to Jermaine himself.
Potential nickname alert
German, Germs, Your Majesty, Your Highness.

Jesus

Origin and meaning
Hebrew origin, meaning 'salvation'.
Jesus Christ led a brief but highly influential life in Roman times. Jesus is a common first name among Hispanic cultures.
Potential nickname alert
Zeus, Big J, Lord.

Kent

Origin and meaning
Old English origin, meaning 'border', referring to a county in southeast England.
Clarke Kent is Superman's alter ego, and Kent Brockman is a news anchor character in the cartoon series *The Simpsons*.
Potential nickname alert
Ken, Kenny, Superman.

Laertes

Origin and meaning

Greek origin, referring to the father of Odysseus in Greek mythology.

In Shakespeare's *Hamlet* Laertes is Ophelia's brother and the son of Polonius.

Potential nickname alert

Lergy.

Launcelot

Origin and meaning

French origin, meaning 'servant'.

Launcelot was one of King Arthur's knights who betrayed the king by living up to his name, so to speak, when it came to the ladies.

Potential nickname alert

Lance, Lotty, Alot.

Lennon

Origin and meaning

Gaelic origin, meaning 'cloak' or 'lover'.

Lennon Gallagher, son of Oasis pop star Liam Gallagher, was named after the former Beatle John Lennon.

Potential nickname alert

Lenny, Len, Lemon, Lenin.

Leonardo

Origin and meaning
Germanic origin, meaning 'strong as a lion'.
A variant of 'Leonard'. Most commonly known for
da Vinci, the Italian Renaissance genius, and
DiCaprio, the American actor.
Potential nickname alert
Leo, Leonard, Lenny.

Leroy

Origin and meaning
French origin, meaning 'the king' (*le roi*).
Leroy is one of the best known characters from the
1980s American television show *Fame*.
Potential nickname alert
Roy, Lee, King.

Lindley

Origin and meaning
Old English origin, meaning 'woodland clearing',
referring originally to one of the English towns of
that name.
Lindley Miller Garrison was the U.S. Secretary of
War between 1913 and 1916.
Potential nickname alert
Linen, Lily.

Lorenzo

Origin and meaning
Italian origin, meaning 'from Laurentum'.
Lorenzo Odone was an ALD patient whose parents
researched a new treatment for his disease and
inspired the film *Lorenzo's Oil*.
Potential nickname alert
Enzo, Lorry, Oily.

Ludovic

Origin and meaning
German origin, meaning 'famous warrior'.
Ludovic Kennedy was a British journalist and
broadcaster who played a part in the abolition of the
death penalty in the UK, and Ludovic Zamenhof
invented the language Esperanto.
Potential nickname alert
Ludo, Ludicrous, Vic.

Lyle

Origin and meaning
French origin, meaning 'island'.
Lyle Lovett is an American country singer who was
briefly married to the actress Julia Roberts in the
1990s.
Potential nickname alert
Lily, Liar.

Macbeth

Origin and meaning
Gaelic origin, meaning 'son of Beth'.
Macbeth was a Scottish king who inspired
Shakespeare's tragedy of the same name, and
MacBeth Sibaya is a South African football player.
Potential nickname alert
Beth, Mac, Big Mac.

Magnum

Origin and meaning
Latin origin, meaning 'great'.
Magnum Pierre was a Swedish dance producer, and
Magnum P.I. was a 1980s American television series
starring Tom Selleck as a private investigator living in
Hawaii.
Potential nickname alert
Maggie, P.I.

Magnus

Origin and meaning
Latin origin, meaning 'great'.
Magnus Magnusson presented the BBC quiz show
Mastermind for 25 years, and Dr. Magnus Pyke was an
eccentric British scientist best known for waving his
arms about wildly as he spoke.
Potential nickname alert
Maggie.

Makepeace

Origin and meaning
English origin, meaning 'to make peace'.
William Makepeace Thackery was a Victorian
novelist famous for *Vanity Fair*, and *Dempsey &
Makepeace* was a 1980s British television detective
series.
Potential nickname alert
Makepiss, Mack.

Marlon

Origin and meaning
French origin, possibly a variant of 'Merlin'.
Marlon Brando was an American actor best known
for his role in the 1972 gangster film *The Godfather*.
Potential nickname alert
Marly.

Marmaduke

Origin and meaning
Gaelic origin, meaning 'servant of St. Maedoc'.
Marmaduke Hussey was a former chairman of the
BBC, and *Marmaduke* is a Great Dane cartoon and
film character.
Potential nickname alert
Marmite, Duke, Marmalade.

Maximilian

Origin and meaning
Latin origin, meaning 'greatest'.
Maximilian was a robot character in the 1979 sci-fi film *The Black Hole*, and Maximilian Schell is an Oscar-winning Swiss actor who is the godfather of Angelina Jolie.
Potential nickname alert
Max, Maximum, Maxi.

Maxwell

Origin and meaning
Old English origin, meaning 'Mack's spring'.
Maxwell Klinger is a fictional character in the American television series *M*A*S*H*, and Maxwell Edison is a character in Paul McCartney's song *Maxwell's Silver Hammer*.
Potential nickname alert
Max, Maxwell House.

Merlin

Origin and meaning
Welsh origin, meaning 'sea fort'.
Most famously the name of the legendary wizard who hung out with King Arthur, but also the name of the 1933 Rolls Royce engine that went on to power the Spitfire and other World War II aircraft.
Potential nickname alert
Wizard, Magician.

Michelangelo

Origin and meaning
Italian origin, meaning 'the angel Michael'.
Michelangelo was a medieval artist known for his
statue of David and for painting the ceiling of the
Sistine Chapel, and Michelangelo is one of the lead
characters in the comic book, cartoon and film series
Teenage Mutant Ninja Turtles.
Potential nickname alert
Michel, Mike, Mickey, Angel.

Milton

Origin and meaning
Old English origin, meaning 'middle settlement'.
Milton Friedman was an influential 20th-century
economist who is credited with formulating the
concept of monetarism.
Potential nickname alert
Milt, Mitty, Milly.

Moby

Origin and meaning
English origin, coined by the writer Herman Melville
as the name of a whale character, Moby Dick, in the
novel of that name. 'Moby' has since come to mean
'enormous'.
Potential nickname alert
Dick, Whale.

Montague

Origin and meaning
French origin, meaning 'pointed hill'.
Montague John Druitt was a Victorian barrister who some believe to have been Jack the Ripper because he killed himself shortly after the last Ripper murder.
Potential nickname alert
Monty.

Montgomery

Origin and meaning
French origin, meaning 'Gomeric's hill'.
Field Marshall Bernard Montgomery fought the Nazis in North Africa during World War II, and Montgomery Burns is the evil billionaire in the cartoon show *The Simpsons*.
Potential nickname alert
Monty, Mr. Burns.

Monty

Origin and meaning
French origin, an abbreviation of 'Montgomery'.
Monty Don is a television gardening expert and Monty Python was the collective name used by comedians John Cleese, Graham Chapman, Michael Palin, Terry Jones, Eric Idle and Terry Gilliam when working together.
Potential nickname alert
Del Monte, Python.

Morgan

Origin and meaning
Welsh origin, meaning 'sea born'.
Morgan is a brand of hand-built, classic style sports
cars, and Morgan Freeman is an Oscar-winning
American actor who has starred in dozens of films
including *The Dark Knight* and *Million Dollar Baby*.
Potential nickname alert
Organ, Moggie.

Moses

Origin and meaning
Egyptian origin, meaning 'water reeds'.
The Biblical Moses is said to have led the Hebrew
people out of Egypt and to have received the Ten
Commandments from God.
Potential nickname alert
Mo, Moss.

Mungo

Origin and meaning
Scottish and Gaelic origin, meaning 'dearest'.
Also the name of the dog character in the early 1970s
children's animation *Mary, Mungo and Midge*.
Potential nickname alert
Mango, Mungie.

Nathanial

Origin and meaning
Hebrew origin, meaning 'gift from God'.
Nathanial Philip Rothschild is a financier who was placed 156th in the *Sunday Times Rich List 2009*, and Nathanial Parker is a British actor who stars in the television series *The Inspector Lynley Mysteries*.
Potential nickname alert
Nathan, Nate, Nat.

Nelson

Origin and meaning
English origin, meaning 'son of Neil'.
Formerly given as a name in honour of Lord Nelson who died during his otherwise victorious Battle of Trafalgar in 1805, it is now better known for its association with Mandela, the former President of South Africa.
Potential nickname alert
Nelly.

Niles

Origin and meaning
African origin, referring to the river Nile.
Niles Crane is the fictional brother of the psychiatrist character Dr. Frasier Crane in the American sitcom *Frasier*.
Potential nickname alert
River, Dr. Crane.

Noah

Origin and meaning
Hebrew origin, meaning 'rest'.
Noah from the Book of Genesis saved pairs of
animals while his god was busy committing
genocide, and Noah Taylor is an Australian actor
who played Mr. Bucket in *Charlie and the Chocolate
Factory*.
Potential nickname alert
No, Ark.

Obadiah

Origin and meaning
Hebrew origin, meaning 'God's servant'.
The character Obadiah Stane was played by Jeff
Bridges in the 2008 film *Iron Man*.
Potential nickname alert
Obie, Baddy.

Octavius

Origin and meaning
Latin origin, meaning 'eight'.
Octavius Caesar was a Roman emperor, and
Octavius Squeezer is a brand of analogue bass pedal
for guitarists.
Potential nickname alert
Octopus, Tavy.

Odysseus

Origin and meaning
Greek origin, meaning 'anger'.
A character from Homer's epic poems, it is also
related to the Latin version of the name, 'Ulysses'.
Potential nickname alert
Oddie, Space Odyssey.

Omar

Origin and meaning
Hebrew origin, meaning 'speaker'.
Since 2004, the American actor Omar Epps has
played the role of Dr. Eric Foreman in the medical
drama series *House*, and Omar Bongo was the
President of Gabon until his death in 2009.
Potential nickname alert
Omargod.

Orlando

Origin and meaning
Italian origin, meaning 'famous land'.
The name was given by Shakespeare to a lead
character in his play *As You Like It*, and it is also
famous as the Florida location for Walt Disney World
and for the actor Orlando Bloom.
Potential nickname alert
Lando, Olly.

Orson

Origin and meaning
Latin origin, meaning 'bear'.
Orson Welles was a film director famous for *Citizen Kane*, and Orson Bean has been an American film and television actor for 60 years.
Potential nickname alert
Ors, Bear, Sonny.

Othello

Origin and meaning
German origin, meaning 'wealth'.
Shakespeare's *Othello* is an African prince battling prejudice in Europe, and there is a popular board game of the same name.
Potential nickname alert
Cello, Yellow.

Otis

Origin and meaning
Greek origin, meaning 'keen hearing'.
Otis Spunkmeyer is a brand of cookies and muffins, and Otis Redding was an American soul singer famous for the posthumous hit *(Sittin' On) The Dock of the Bay*.
Potential nickname alert
Otie, Oats.

Otto

Origin and meaning
German origin, meaning 'wealth'.
The aristocrat Otto von Bismark became the first
Chancellor of the German Empire in 1871, and Otto
Preminger was an American film director who made
more than 35 films in his career.
Potential nickname alert
Otter, Ottomatic.

Paddington

Origin and meaning
Anglo-Saxon origin, meaning the 'estate of Padda'.
Now more commonly associated with a railway
station and a fictional Peruvian bear with a penchant
for marmalade sandwiches.
Potential nickname alert
Bear, Teddy, Station.

Percival

Origin and meaning
French origin, meaning 'pierce the valley'.
Percival was one of King Arthur's legendary Knights
of the Round Table, and Percival Lowell was an
astronomer who caused concern in the early 20th-
century when he discovered 'evidence' of intelligent
life on Mars.
Potential nickname alert
Percy.

Pericles

Origin and meaning
Greek origin, meaning 'widely famous'.
Pericles was an influential statesman in ancient
Greece, known as the 'first citizen of Athens'. Pericles
Snowdon is an up-and-coming young London
playwright.
Potential nickname alert
Perry.

Phineas

Origin and meaning
Hebrew origin, meaning 'oracle'.
Phineas Fogg is the lead character in the novel *Around
the World in 80 Days* by Jules Verne, and *Phineas and
Ferb* is an American cartoon show.
Potential nickname alert
Fin, Pin.

Preston

Origin and meaning
Old English origin, meaning 'priest's town'.
The character Preston Burke appeared in the
television show *Grey's Anatomy*, and Preston Blair was
an American animator who worked at the Disney
studios in the 1930s.
Potential nickname alert
Presto, Pest.

Prince

Origin and meaning

Latin origin, meaning 'son of royalty'.
Prince Jackson is Michael Jackson's eldest son, and
Clive Prince is a bestselling esoteric author whose
writings were part of the inspiration behind the novel
The Da Vinci Code.

Potential nickname alert

Princess, Your Highness, Your Majesty.

Quentin

Origin and meaning

Latin origin, meaning 'fifth'.
The name is well represented in the Arts with author
Quentin Crisp, film director Quentin Tarantino and
artist Quentin Blake.

Potential nickname alert

Quen.

Quincy

Origin and meaning

Latin origin, meaning 'fifth'.
Quincy Jones is an American record producer famous
for his work with Michael Jackson and Frank Sinatra,
and *Quincy M.E.* was an American medical-detective
television show in the 1970s and 1980s.

Potential nickname alert

Quince, Quinny.

Rameses

Origin and meaning

Egyptian origin, meaning 'son of Ra' (sometimes
spelled 'Ramses' or 'Ramesses').

Rameses was the name of a number of 19th- and
20th-Dynasty Egyptian pharaohs, and is also the
name of a brand of condom.

Potential nickname alert

Rambo, Ram.

Redmond

Origin and meaning

German origin, meaning 'protector'.

Redmond O'Neal is the son of actors Ryan O'Neal
and Farrah Fawcett, and Phil Redmond created the
British television series *Grange Hill*.

Potential nickname alert

Red, Reddy.

Reuben

Origin and meaning

Hebrew origin, meaning 'all look: a son!'

Reuben Fine was an American chess champion, and a
Reuben sandwich is a meal containing corned beef,
sauerkraut and Swiss cheese with grilled bread.

Potential nickname alert

Tuby, Rhubarb, Booben.

Rhys

Origin and meaning
Welsh origin, meaning 'enthusiasm'.
The Welsh actor Rhys Ifans rose to fame in the film
Notting Hill, and the New Zealand comedian and
actor Rhys Darby is best known for playing the band
manager Murray Hewitt in *Flight of the Conchords*.
Potential nickname alert
Rice, Piss.

Ringo

Origin and meaning
English origin, meaning 'ring'.
The drummer Richard Starkey chose the name
Ringo Starr before being picked in 1962 to replace
Pete Best in a pop group called The Beatles.
Potential nickname alert
Bingo, Dingo.

Rocco

Origin and meaning
Italian origin, meaning 'rock'.
Rocco Barker was a member of 1980s rock bands
Flesh for Lulu and Wasted Youth, and Rocco Ritchie
is the son of Madonna and Guy Ritchie.
Potential nickname alert
Rocky.

Rock

Origin and meaning
English origin, a variant of the Italian 'Rocco'.
Rock Hudson was the stage name of Roy Scherer,
who starred in many films of the 1950s and 1960s.
Potential nickname alert
Rocky, Rocco.

Rocky

Origin and meaning
English origin, a variant of the Italian 'Rocco'.
The name is intrinsically linked with the sport of
boxing due to the fame of the real life boxer Rocky
Marciano and the fictional champ Rocky Balboa.
Potential nickname alert
Rocco, Bulwinkle, Balboa.

Rollo

Origin and meaning
German origin, meaning 'famous land', a variant of
'Roland'.
Rollo Armstrong is a music producer and is the older
brother of the pop star Dido, and Rollo Weeks is a
Chichester-born actor who starred alongside Patrick
Swayze in the 2004 film *George and the Dragon*.
Potential nickname alert
Roland, Rolly, Brillo.

Romeo

Origin and meaning
Italian origin, meaning 'Roman citizen'.
Best known as a lead character in Shakespeare's
tragedy *Romeo and Juliet*, as well as being Brooklyn
Beckham's brother.
Potential nickname alert
Homeo, Rome, Romy.

Rudyard

Origin and meaning
Old English origin, meaning 'red garden'.
The name is best known for the Indian-born author
of the exceedingly good *The Jungle Book*.
Potential nickname alert
Rudy, Rud.

Rufus

Origin and meaning
Latin origin, meaning 'redhead'.
Rufus Sewell is an English actor who recently starred
in the US television series *Eleventh Hour* and Rufus
Wainwright is a Canadian-American singer-
songwriter.
Potential nickname alert
Roof, Rufie.

Saddam

Origin and meaning
Arabic origin, meaning 'brave'.
Made notorious by the former Iraqi dictator Saddam Hussein.
Potential nickname alert
Hussein, WMD.

Samson

Origin and meaning
Hebrew origin, meaning 'sun'.
The name is associated with superhuman strength (and long hair) thanks to the Bible story of Samson and Delilah.
Potential nickname alert
Sam, Sammy, Samsung.

Septimus

Origin and meaning
Latin origin, meaning 'seventh'.
This name was often given to the seventh child to be born in a family. *Septimus Heap* is a series of fantasy novels written by the British author Angie Sage.
Potential nickname alert
Seppy, Tim, Timus.

Sextus

Origin and meaning
Latin origin, meaning 'sixth'.
A common name in Roman times, but has slipped
almost completely off the radar since. Sextus is a
minor fictional character in the novel and film
Stardust.
Potential nickname alert
Sexy.

Sherman

Origin and meaning
Old English origin, meaning 'cloth cutter'.
Sherman Klump is the lead character played by Eddie
Murphy in the comedy films *The Nutty Professor* and
Nutty Professor II: The Klumps.
Potential nickname alert
Sperman, Sherm.

Shylock

Origin and meaning
Shakespearean origin, referring to the Jewish
moneylender in *The Merchant of Venice* who insists on
a 'pound of flesh' as collateral against the money
loaned to Antonio.
Potential nickname alert
Shyster, Shy.

Silas

Origin and meaning
Latin origin, meaning 'forest'.
Silas is an albino monk character in the novel *The Da Vinci Code*, and Silas Marner is the protagonist in George Eliot's novel of that name.
Potential nickname alert
Silage, Sinus.

Sophocles

Origin and meaning
Greek origin, referring to the ancient Greek writer of tragic plays such as *Oedipus Rex* and *Antigone*.
Sophocles is the name of the first son of *Flight of the Conchords* star Jemaine Clement.
Potential nickname alert
Sophie, Soppy.

Stafford

Origin and meaning
Old English origin, meaning 'ford with a landing place'.
The American actor Stafford Repp played the role of Chief O'Hara in the 1960s *Batman* television series.
Potential nickname alert
Staffy, Staff, Stifford.

Stalin

Origin and meaning
Russian origin, meaning 'steel'.
Surname of the 20th-century Soviet dictator who
established the 'Iron Curtain' across Europe and
began the Cold War.
Potential nickname alert
Lynn, Star.

Taggart

Origin and meaning
Gaelic origin, meaning 'priest's son'.
Taggart is the name of a Scottish television detective
show as well as the name of a character in the spoof
American western film *Blazing Saddles*.
Potential nickname alert
Taggers.

Talbot

Origin and meaning
Germanic origin, meaning 'messenger of destruction'.
Talbot is a defunct brand of mediocre cars, and Talbot
Mundy was a British writer of adventure stories.
Potential nickname alert
Horizon, Bot.

Theodore

Origin and meaning
Greek origin, meaning 'gift of God'.
Best known as the first name of President Roosevelt
who, in the early 20th century, is said to have been
the inspiration for the concept of a 'teddy bear'.
Potential nickname alert
Theo, Ted, Teddy.

Thor

Origin and meaning
Norse origin, meaning 'thunder'.
Thor Schenker is a French actor and singer, and Thor
Heyerdahl was a Norwegian explorer famous for his
Kon-Tiki Expedition.
Potential nickname alert
Whore, Door.

Tiger

Origin and meaning
English origin, referring to the big cat found in South
East Asia.
Tiger Woods is an American golf champion, and
Tiger Onitsuka is a Japanese jazz drummer.
Potential nickname alert
Tigger.

Tito

Origin and meaning
Latin and Greek origin, meaning 'of the giants'.
Tito Jackson was an original member of the American
singing group The Jackson Five.
Potential nickname alert
Tits, Titty.

Tygert

Origin and meaning
American origin, referring to a West Virginian river
and lake.
Tygert Pennington (better known as 'Ty') is the
American presenter of the reality television show
Extreme Makeover: Home Edition.
Potential nickname alert
Tiger.

Tyler

Origin and meaning
Old English origin, meaning 'tile maker' or 'tile
layer'.
Tyler Perry is an American writer, actor and director
who is reputed to be one of the highest-earning
people in Hollywood.
Potential nickname alert
Ty.

Tyrone

Origin and meaning
Gaelic origin, referring to the ancient Northern Ireland kingdom of Tir Eogain, now known as County Tyrone.
Tyrone Power was an early 20th-century American actor who played lead roles in swashbuckling films such as *The Mask of Zorro*.

Potential nickname alert
Tizer, Ty.

Tutankhamun

Origin and meaning
Egyptian origin, meaning 'the living image of Amun'. King Tutankhamun reigned Egypt during his teenage years, then languished in obscurity for more than 3,000 years waiting for Howard Carter to dig him up and make him famous again.

Potential nickname alert
Tut, King Tut, Tanky, Tutan.

Ulysses

Origin and meaning
Latin origin, a variant of the Greek name 'Odysseus' meaning 'anger'.
Ulysses is a 'stream of consciousness' novel by Irish author James Joyce, and in 1869 Ulysses S. Grant became the 18th President of the United States.

Potential nickname alert
Useless, Ollie.

Umberto

Origin and meaning
German origin, meaning 'famous giant'.
Umberto Eco is an Italian novelist, and Umberto
Giordano was an Italian operatic composer.
Potential nickname alert
Umbrella, Dumbo.

Walter

Origin and meaning
German origin, meaning 'military commander'.
The name is associated with the mariner Sir Walter
Raleigh, news anchor Walter Cronkite and animator
Walt Disney.
Potential nickname alert
Wally, Walt.

Wenceslas

Origin and meaning
Slavic origin, meaning 'greater glory'.
Good King Wenceslas is a popular Christmas carol,
based on the story of St. Wenceslas, 10th-century
Duke of Bohemia.
Potential nickname alert
Good King, Wendy.

Wolfgang

Origin and meaning
German origin, meaning 'wolf path'.
Wolfgang Amadeus Mozart was the 18th-century
prodigal Austrian composer who created more than
600 musical works.
Potential nickname alert
Wolfie, Foxy.

Woody

Origin and meaning
English origin, a variant of 'Woodrow' meaning 'row
of houses by a wood'.
Woody Allen is an American actor, comedian and
director, and Woody Harrelson is an American actor
who rose to fame in the sitcom *Cheers*.
Potential nickname alert
Woodpecker.

Xerxes

Origin and meaning
Persian origin, meaning 'king'.
Xerxes Cook is a journalist who has written for *The
Guardian* newspaper, and Xerxes the Great became
King of Persia in 486 BC.
Potential nickname alert
Jerkxes, X.

Yorick

Origin and meaning
Old English origin, meaning 'farmer'.
Yorick is a fictional court jester whose skull appears in
Shakespeare's *Hamlet*, and Yorick Wilks is a Professor
of Artificial Intelligence at the University of
Sheffield.
Potential nickname alert
Alas Poor, Yo-yo.

Zacharia

Origin and meaning
Hebrew origin, meaning 'God has remembered'.
Also spelt Zachariah. Zachariah Selwyn is an
American singer-songwriter known for his
appearances on reality television shows.
Potential nickname alert
Zac, Zacky.

Zane

Origin and meaning
Hebrew origin, meaning 'God is gracious'.
Zane Truesdale is a fictional duelist character in the
Japanese cartoon series *Yu-Gi-Oh!*
Potential nickname alert
Zany, Inzane.

Zebedee

Origin and meaning
Hebrew origin, meaning 'gift of God'.
Zebedee is a bizarre spring-loaded character from the children's television animation *The Magic Roundabout*.
Potential nickname alert
Zeb, Dee.

Zeus

Origin and meaning
Greek origin, referring to the Greek god considered to be the ruler of all of gods, and who can be found living at an address in Mount Olympus.
Potential nickname alert
Zoo, Sauce.

Ziggy

Origin and meaning
Hebrew origin, a variant of 'Zachary' and 'Zacharia'.
Ziggy Stardust is a David Bowie song and Ziggy Lichman was a contestant in the UK television show *Big Brother* in 2007.
Potential nickname alert
Zig-Zag, Ziggers.

Unusual Names
for Girls

Agnes

Origin and meaning
Greek origin, meaning 'pure, holy and chaste'.
Its unglamorous reputation is surely due for a reversal
in this age of irony. Agnes Moorehead was an
American actress who played Endora in the sitcom
Bewitched.
Potential nickname alert
Aggie, Nes, Angus.

Aislinn

Origin and meaning
Gaelic origin, meaning 'dream'.
Aislinn Laing is a reporter for the *Daily Telegraph*, and
Aislinn O'Sullivan is the former wife of Irish rock
singer The Edge.
Potential nickname alert
Ace, Lynn, Alison.

Alissa

Origin and meaning
Greek origin, meaning 'rational'.
Alissa Czisny is an American champion figure skater,
Alissa Firsova is a Russian-born composer, and Alissa
York is a Canadian novelist.
Potential nickname alert
Lisa, Ali.

Allegra

Origin and meaning
Italian origin, meaning 'happy'.
Allegra Versace is the daughter of Italian designer
Donatella Versace, and Allegra Byron was the
illegitimate daughter of the poet Lord Byron.
Potential nickname alert
Ally, Aggro.

Amélie

Origin and meaning
Greek origin, meaning 'friendly'.
Amélie Mauresmo is a French champion tennis
player, and Amélie Poulain is the fictional protagonist
of the French film *Amélie* starring Audrey Tautou.
Potential nickname alert
Amy, Emily.

America

Origin and meaning
Germanic origin meaning 'strong in battle'.
America Olivo is an American actress and model, and
America Ferrera is an American actress who stars in
the television series *Ugly Betty*.
Potential nickname alert
Ugly Betty, Yank.

Apple

Origin and meaning
Simply named after the healthy fruit, it was a
common name historically but is rarely used today.
Apple is the daughter of Gwyneth Paltrow and Chris
Martin, and Apple Miyuki is a Japanese professional
wrestler.
Potential nickname alert
Cider, Pie.

April

Origin and meaning
Latin origin, meaning 'to open' (referring to the
opening of flowers in spring).
April Bowlby is an American actress best known for
her role in the sitcom *Two and a Half Men*.
Potential nickname alert
Ape, Fool.

Arabella

Origin and meaning
Latin origin, meaning 'beautiful'.
Arabella Weir is a British comedian, writer and actress
best known for *The Fast Show*, and *Arabella* is an opera
by Richard Strauss.
Potential nickname alert
Arab, Bella, Ella, Umbrella.

Arianna

Origin and meaning
Greek origin, meaning 'most holy'.
Arianna Huffington is a Greek American journalist who stood against Arnold Schwarzenegger for the governorship of California in 2003.
Potential nickname alert
Ariola, Ari, Anna, Airy.

Aurelia

Origin and meaning
Latin origin, meaning 'golden'.
Aurelia Cotta was the mother of Julius Caesar, and Aurelia Tizón was the first wife of Argentinian President Juan Perón (she died some years before Evita came on the scene).
Potential nickname alert
Relia, Lia, Aurie, Australia.

Barbie

Origin and meaning
Latin origin, a variant of 'Barbara' meaning 'foreigner'.
Barbie is a brand of fashion doll, Barbie Hsu is a Taiwanese actress and Klaus Barbie was a Nazi war criminal.
Potential nickname alert
Barb, Babs, Doll.

Bathsheba

Origin and meaning
Hebrew origin, meaning 'daughter of the oath'.
Bathsheba Everdene is the fictional heroine of
Thomas Hardy's novel *Far from the Madding Crowd*,
and Bathsheba Doran is a British playwright living in
New York.
Potential nickname alert
Bath, Sheba, Queen of Sheba.

Belladonna

Origin and meaning
Italian origin, meaning 'beautiful lady'.
Belladonna Baggins is the fictional mother of Bilbo
Baggins in J.R.R. Tolkein's novels *The Hobbit* and
The Lord of the Rings.
Potential nickname alert
Bella, Donna, Belly.

Bernadette

Origin and meaning
German origin, meaning 'brave as a bear', the female
version of 'Bernard'.
Bernadette Chirac is the wife of the former French
President, Jacques Chirac, and Bernadette Peters is an
American film and television actress.
Potential nickname alert
Bernard, Bernie, Bern.

Betty Kitten

Origin and meaning
Betty comes from various origins, including Dutch, English, Greek and Hebrew, and means 'holy promise'.
Kitten is self-explanatory. Chat show king Jonathon Ross gave this name to his eldest daughter.
Potential nickname alert
Betty Boop, Ugly Betty, Kitty.

Beyoncé

Origin and meaning
English origin, made famous by the bestselling American singer-songwriter Beyoncé Knowles.
Potential nickname alert
Bee, Destiny's Child.

Bianca

Origin and meaning
Italian origin, meaning 'white' or 'pure'.
Bianca Jackson is a fictional character in the British soap opera *EastEnders*, and Bianca Jagger is the former wife of Rolling Stone singer Mick Jagger.
Potential nickname alert
Bee, Bibi, Binky.

Bidisha

Origin and meaning
Indian origin, meaning 'knowledge'.
Bidisha is a British writer and presenter who had her
first novel published at the age of 16, and recently
published a travel memoir *Venetian Masters*.
Potential nickname alert
Dish, Disha, Bidi.

Bluebell

Origin and meaning
English origin, meaning a type of blue flower.
The bluebell is the national flower of Scotland, and
Geri Halliwell named her daughter Bluebell
Madonna.
Potential nickname alert
Bluey, Bell, Bella.

Boadicea

Origin and meaning
English origin, meaning 'triumphant'.
Boadicea was a legendary East Anglian queen who led
a massive revolt against the Romans. Recently
historians have questioned the spelling of 'Boadicea',
and concluded that 'Boudica' is more probably
correct.
Potential nickname alert
Boady.

Buttercup

Origin and meaning
English origin, meaning 'flower'.
Buttercup is the name of the female protagonist in the novel and film *The Princess Bride*, and the name of one of the lead characters in the American children's animation *The Powerpuff Girls*.
Potential nickname alert
Butters, Butt, Tea Cup.

Butterfly

Origin and meaning
English origin, meaning 'a bright coloured flying insect'.
Butterfly McQueen was an American actress who appeared in the 1939 film *Gone with the Wind*.
Potential nickname alert
Butters, Butt, Caterpillar.

Calypso

Origin and meaning
Greek origin, meaning 'name of a sea nymph'.
Calypso was the name of Jacques Cousteau's ship, a John Denver song, and a character in the Mary Wesley novel and television series *The Camomile Lawn*.
Potential nickname alert
Cally, Lips.

Camera

Origin and meaning
Arabic origin, meaning 'dark room with a small window'.
Camera Ashe is the daughter of the late tennis champion Arthur Ashe.
Potential nickname alert
Cam, Flash, Digital.

Candy

Origin and meaning
Latin origin, meaning 'whiteness' (a form of 'Candice').
Candy Clark is an American actress who starred in the George Lucas film *American Graffiti*, and Candy ('Candice') Bergen is an American actress famous for her role in the television series *Boston Legal*.
Potential nickname alert
Candice, Sugar.

Carmelita

Origin and meaning
Hebrew origin, meaning 'from Mount Carmel'.
Carmelita Jeter is an American athlete, and Carmelita Spats is a fictional character in series of children's novels, *A Series of Unfortunate Events*.
Potential nickname alert
Caramel, Camel, Mel.

Carmen

Origin and meaning

Latin and Spanish origin meaning 'song', making it an appropriate title for a Bizet opera and for the heroine of the story.

Carmen Miranda was a Brazilian samba singer famous for wearing fruit on her head.

Potential nickname alert

Carmie, Car.

Catriona

Origin and meaning

Greek origin, meaning 'pure', one of many variants of the name 'Catherine'.

Catriona McPherson is a British crime novelist, and Catriona Morrison is a British medal-winning triathlete and duathlete.

Potential nickname alert

Cat, Katy, Kitty, Triona.

Champagne

Origin and meaning

French origin, referring to the region in France where sparkling wine is produced for sale at premium prices.

Victoria Champagne Sutherland is an American publisher of *ForeWord Reviews* magazine.

Potential nickname alert

Bubbly, Shampoo.

Chardonnay

Origin and meaning
French origin, meaning 'thistle-covered place', most commonly associated with a variety of white wine. Chardonnay Lane-Pascoe is a fictional character in the British television series *Footballers' Wives*.
Potential nickname alert
Charlie, Char, Donnay.

Charis

Origin and meaning
Greek origin, meaning 'charm'.
Charis Wilson was an American photographic model, and Charis LeeAnn is an American soul music singer and songwriter.
Potential nickname alert
Carrie, Chas.

Charisma

Origin and meaning
Greek origin, meaning 'charm'.
Charisma Carpenter is an American actress who played Cordelia Chase in the televisions series *Buffy the Vampire Slayer*.
Potential nickname alert
Charis, Chrissy, Carrie.

Charity

Origin and meaning
Latin origin, meaning 'benevolence'.
Charity Shea is an American actress, and Charity
Bazaar is a character in the American children's
animation series *Histeria!*
Potential nickname alert
Cherry, Chas.

Chastity

Origin and meaning
Latin origin, meaning 'pure'.
Chastity Bono is the daughter (currently undergoing
surgery to become the son) of American singers
Sonny and Cher, and Chastity Dingle is a character in
the British soap opera *Emmerdale*.
Potential nickname alert
Chas, Titty, Belt.

Chelsea

Origin and meaning
English origin, meaning 'chalk wharf'.
Chelsea Clinton is the daughter of former U.S.
President Bill Clinton, Chelsea Georgeson is an
Australian champion surfer, and Chelsea Cooley is a
former Miss USA.
Potential nickname alert
Chel, Clinton.

Cheryl

Origin and meaning
French origin, meaning 'darling'.
Cheryl Cole is a British singer and talent show judge, and Cheryl Baker is a British singer who won the *Eurovision Song Contest* in 1981 as part of the band *Bucks Fizz*.
Potential nickname alert
Cher, Cherry, Beryl.

Cherry

Origin and meaning
Latin origin, referring to the Roman place from which cherries were first exported.
Cherry Chevapravatdumrong is an American writer of episodes of the cartoon series *Family Guy*.
Potential nickname alert
Cher, Chez, Cheery.

Cinderella

Origin and meaning
French origin, meaning 'ash girl'.
Cinderella is a fairy tale that originated in ancient Egypt and spread worldwide over many centuries.
Cinderella Gatcheco is an American actress.
Potential nickname alert
Cinders, Sin, Cindy.

Cleopatra

Origin and meaning

Greek origin, meaning 'father's glory'.

This name was given to several queens of ancient Egypt, of which Cleopatra VII is best known to us thanks to Shakespeare's dramatisation of her milky relationship with Mark Anthony.

Potential nickname alert

Cleo, Pat.

Coco

Origin and meaning

French origin, has no special meaning other than the sound made by parrots and is hence a common name for these avian pets in France.

Coco Cox Arquette is the daughter of American actress Courtney Cox, and Coco Chanel was a famous fashion designer.

Potential nickname alert

Coco Pops, Coco Puffs, Coke.

Condoleezza

Origin and meaning

Italian origin, meaning 'with sweetness'.

Dr. Condoleezza Rice was the United States National Security Advisor from 2001 to 2005, and Secretary of State from 2005 to 2009.

Potential nickname alert

Connie, Condo, Lisa, Condom.

Cymbeline

Origin and meaning
Greek origin, meaning 'hollow'.
Cymbeline is the title of a Shakespeare play, and
Cymbeline Smith is a British actress who appeared in
the 2008 film *Strange Angel*.
Potential nickname alert
Cymbal, Sim, Bella.

Daffodil

Origin and meaning
Greek origin, from the legend of Narcissus in which a
daffodil grows on the spot where a vain boy died after
staring at his own reflection in the water for too long.
Potential nickname alert
Daffy Duck.

Daisy

Origin and meaning
English origin, meaning 'the sun' (from the old
English word for 'day's eye').
Daisy Duke is a character in the 1970s American
television show *The Dukes of Hazzard*, and Daisy Boo
Oliver is the daughter of chef Jamie Oliver.
Potential nickname alert
Daze, Lazy, Crazy.

Dandelion

Origin and meaning
French origin, meaning 'lion's tooth'.
Dandelion is a character in the novel and film
Watership Down, and Dandelion Richards is the
daughter of Rolling Stone guitarist Keith Richards.
Potential nickname alert
Dandy, Lion.

Darleen

Origin and meaning
English origin, meaning 'darling'.
Darleen Carr is an American actress and Darleen
Zavaroni is the cousin of singer Lena Zavaroni.
Potential nickname alert
Darling, Lena.

Deirdre

Origin and meaning
Gaelic origin, meaning 'sad'.
In Irish folklore Deirdre was the country's most
beautiful woman. The name lost popularity
following its use in Monty Python's famous
'Vocational Guidance Councillor' sketch which made
it sound like the most drab and dull name possible.
Potential nickname alert
Dee, Dee-Dee, Dreary, Weirdre.

Delilah

Origin and meaning
Hebrew origin, meaning 'slim' or 'seductive'.
In the Bible story, Delilah cut off Samson's hair to
remove his strength. It was also the title of a hit song
for Tom Jones in 1968.
Potential nickname alert
Lila, Lily, Deli.

Desdemona

Origin and meaning
Greek origin, meaning 'unfortunate'.
Desdemona is a Venetian character in Shakespeare's
play *Othello*, and is also a Texan town and the name of
a moon of Uranus.
Potential nickname alert
Des, Mona.

Destiny

Origin and meaning
Latin origin, meaning 'fate'.
Destiny Angel is a character in the 1960s children's
puppet television series *Captain Scarlet and the
Mysterons*.
Potential nickname alert
Des, Destiny's Child, Tiny.

Dinah

Origin and meaning
Hebrew origin, meaning 'judged'.
Dinah Sheridan is a British actress who played the
mother in the 1970 film *The Railway Children*, and
Dinah Morris is a fictional character in George Eliot's
novel *Adam Bede*.
Potential nickname alert
Dee, Dynamite, Dynamo.

Dora

Origin and meaning
Greek origin, meaning 'God's gift'.
Dora Bryan is a British actress best known for her role
in the sitcom *Last of the Summer Wine*, and *Dora the
Explorer* is an educational children's cartoon show.
Potential nickname alert
Dorie, Dodo, Door.

Eadgyth

Origin and meaning
English origin, meaning 'prosperity in battle' or
'Edith of England', referring to the granddaughter of
King Alfred the Great who went to Germany to
marry the Duke of Saxony in 929.
Potential nickname alert
Edith.

Eartha

Origin and meaning
Gaelic origin, meaning 'strong belief'.
Eartha Kitt was an American singer and actress best
known for her role as Catwoman in the 1960s
television series *Batman*.
Potential nickname alert
Mud, Clod, Soil, Arthur.

Ebony

Origin and meaning
Greek origin, meaning 'black wood'.
Ebony Thomas, better known as Ebony Bones, is a
British singer-songwriter and actress who appeared in
the soap opera *Family Affairs*.
Potential nickname alert
Eb, Bony, Ivory.

Emmanuelle

Origin and meaning
Hebrew origin, meaning 'God is with us'.
Emmanuelle Vaugier is a Canadian actress best known
for her role in the television series *CSI: New York*, and
Emmanuelle is an iconic adult film from the 1970s.
Potential nickname alert
Emma, Manuel.

Emmeline

Origin and meaning
German origin, meaning 'whole' or 'universal'. Emmeline Pankhurst was a leading British suffragette in the early 20th century, and Emmeline Brice was the oldest living person in Britain when she died in 2006 at the age of 111.
Potential nickname alert
Em, Emma, Emmie.

Ermintrude

Origin and meaning
Germanic origin, meaning 'courageous in battle'. Best known as the matronly, flower-eating bovine character from the children's television show *The Magic Roundabout*.
Potential nickname alert
Trudy.

Evita

Origin and meaning
Hebrew origin, meaning 'life' (a variant of 'Eve'). *Evita* is the title of a musical and film based on the short life of Eva Perón, wife of the former Argentinian President Juan Perón.
Potential nickname alert
Eve, Eva, Don't Cry For Me.

Faith

Origin and meaning
Latin origin, meaning 'trust'.
Faith Evans is an American singer, and Faith Brown is a British comedienne and impressionist who rose to fame in the 1970s.
Potential nickname alert
Fay, Fido.

Fenella

Origin and meaning
Gaelic origin, meaning 'fair shouldered'.
Fenella Fudge is a BBC radio news reader, and Fenella Woolgar is a British actress who has appeared in films such as *Bright Young Things* and *St Trinian's*.
Potential nickname alert
Fen, Nelly, Vanilla.

Fifi

Origin and meaning
Hebrew origin, meaning 'God increases' (a variant of 'Josephine').
Fifi Trixibelle is the daughter of Bob Geldof and Paula Yates, and Fifi D'Orsay was a Canadian actress who starred in many films during the 1930s.
Potential nickname alert
Fi, Fifty, Iffy.

Florence

Origin and meaning
Latin origin, meaning 'flowering'.
Florence Nightingale was named after the Italian city where she was born, and Florence Henderson is an American actress who played Carol Brady in the sitcom *The Brady Bunch*.
Potential nickname alert
Flo, Flossie, Machine.

Frogmella

Origin and meaning
English origin, meaning 'ugly woman'.
Frogmella Slob is a fictional baby character in the 1990s British television sketch shows *Harry Enfield's Television Programme* and *Harry Enfield and Chums*.
Potential nickname alert
Frog, Froggie.

Fuchsia

Origin and meaning
Name given in 1703 to a species of magenta flower by the French botanist Charles Plumier, who named it after the 16th-century German botanist Leonhart Fuchs.
Fuchsia is also the name of the daughter of the British singer Sting.
Potential nickname alert
Fuchwit, Flower, Fuchs.

Georgy Girl

Origin and meaning
Greek origin, meaning 'farmer'.
Georgy Girl is a 1966 British film starring Lynn
Redgrave, the theme song of which sparked a number
one hit for The Seekers.
Potential nickname alert
George, Georgina, GeeGee.

Gertrude

Origin and meaning
Germanic origin, meaning 'strong spear'.
Shakespeare's Queen Gertrude is Hamlet's mother,
and Gertrude Jekyll was a British garden designer.
Potential nickname alert
Gerty, Trudy.

Grace

Origin and meaning
Latin origin, meaning 'pleasing'.
Grace Kelly was an American actress who married
Prince Rainier of Monaco, and Grace Mugabe is the
second wife of President Robert Mugabe of
Zimbabwe.
Potential nickname alert
Gracy, Grey, Amazing.

Greta

Origin and meaning
Greek origin, meaning 'pearl' (a variant of 'Margaret').
Greta Garbo was a Swedish actress who became an early Hollywood star, and Greta Bösel was a Nazi concentration camp guard who in 1947 was hanged for her crimes.
Potential nickname alert
Gretel, Hansel, Great.

Guinevere

Origin and meaning
Gaelic origin, meaning 'white ghost'.
Guinevere was the legendary queen of King Arthur, who reputedly betrayed him by having an affair with Sir Launcelot.
Potential nickname alert
Guin, Pengiun.

Gwendolyn

Origin and meaning
Gaelic origin, meaning 'fair hair'.
Gwendolyn Watts was a British actress who appeared in television sitcoms of the 1960s and 1970s such as *The Rag Trade*, *Steptoe and Son*, and *On the Buses*.
Potential nickname alert
Gwen, Wendy, Lynn.

Heidi

Origin and meaning
German origin, meaning 'noble'.
Heidi, the story of a Swiss orphan, was first published
in 1880 and adapted many times to television and
film, and in 1987 Heidi Stelling was the first test tube
baby to be born in Australia.
Potential nickname alert
Hi, Hi-de-hi.

Hermione

Origin and meaning
Greek origin, meaning 'messenger'.
Hermione Granger is a fictional character in the *Harry
Potter* series of books and films, and Hermione
Cockburn is a British television presenter and writer.
Potential nickname alert
Hermy, Hermit, Minnie.

Himalaya

Origin and meaning
Sanskrit origin, meaning 'the home of snow'.
The Himalayan mountain range is the highest in the
world and includes Mount Everest.
Potential nickname alert
Him, Laya, Everest.

Hippolyta

Origin and meaning
Greek origin, meaning 'stampeding horses'.
In Greek legend, Hippolyta was an Amazonian
queen, and the name also appears in Shakespeare's
acid trip masterpiece *A Midsummer Night's Dream*.
Potential nickname alert
Hippo.

Hope

Origin and meaning
English origin, meaning 'to want'.
Hope Dworaczyk is an American Playboy model, and
Hope Sandoval is an American singer-songwriter.
Potential nickname alert
Hopeless, Hoppy.

Ianthe

Origin and meaning
Greek origin, meaning 'violet'.
Ianthe Fullager won £7 million on the lottery at the
age of 18 whilst still a student, and Ianthe Butt is a
British journalist.
Potential nickname alert
Ian, Anthea.

Isis

Origin and meaning
Ancient Egyptian origin, meaning 'queen', also
known as the Goddess of fertility.
Isis Gee is an American singer who represented
Poland in the 2008 *Eurovision Song Contest*, coming
second to last.
Potential nickname alert
Ice, Iris.

Isolde

Origin and meaning
Celtic origin, meaning 'fair lady'.
In Arthurian legend, Isolde was an Irish princess who
was in love with the knight Tristan, and Isolde
Menges was a 20th-century British violinist.
Potential nickname alert
Izzy, Oldie.

Jacquetta

Origin and meaning
Hebrew origin, meaning 'God will protect'.
Jacquetta Szathmari is an American comedienne and
screenwriter, and Jacquetta Wheeler is a British
model.
Potential nickname alert
Jacqui, Potato.

Jameela

Origin and meaning
Arab origin, meaning 'beautiful'.
Jameela Jamil is a British television presenter, and
Jameela Lares is an American author.
Potential nickname alert
Jam, Jammie, Jemima.

Janna

Origin and meaning
Hebrew origin, meaning 'God is gracious'.
Janna Kramer is an American actress, and Janna Levin
is a cosmologist and author of the award-winning
historical novel *A Madman Dreams of Turing Machines*.
Potential nickname alert
Jan, Jay, Janana.

Jazz

Origin and meaning
Persian origin, a variant of 'Jasmine' referring to the
flower of that name.
Jazz Domino Holly Mellor is the eldest daughter of
punk musician Joe Strummer.
Potential nickname alert
Jazzy, Jizz.

Jinx

Origin and meaning
English origin, meaning 'bringer of bad luck' or 'evil magic spell'.
Jinx Falkenburg was a Spanish-born actress and model who became a pin-up favourite of American troops in World War II.
Potential nickname alert
Jinxie, Jinnie.

Joleen

Origin and meaning
Hebrew origin, a variant of 'Joseph' meaning 'God will add'.
Joleen is the protagonist in the 2008 film *Sleepwalking*, starring Charlize Theron, and, with a slightly different spelling, *Jolene* was a hit for Dolly Parton in 1974.
Potential nickname alert
Jo, Jo Jo, Dolly Parton.

Katia

Origin and meaning
Greek origin, meaning 'pure', a variant of 'Katherine'.
Katia Ivanova is a Kazakhstan-born model famous for dating Rolling Stone guitarist Ronnie Wood, and Katia Milani is a Brazilian-born former model and film producer.
Potential nickname alert
Kat, Katy, Caca.

Kaya

Origin and meaning

Japanese origin, meaning 'excellent'.
Kaya Scodelario is a British actress best known for her
role in the television drama *Skins*, and *Kaya* is the title
of an album recorded by Bob Marley and the Wailers
in 1978.

Potential nickname alert

Kay, Kayak, Maya.

Kendra

Origin and meaning

Celtic origin, meaning 'high hill'.
Kendra Young is a character in the American
television series *Buffy the Vampire Slayer*, and Kendra
Dumbledore is a minor character in the *Harry Potter*
novels.

Potential nickname alert

Ken, Kenny.

Lark Song

Origin and meaning

English origin, meaning 'bird song'.
Lark Song Previn was the name given to a
Vietnamese child who was adopted as the daughter of
actress Mia Farrow and conductor André Previn.

Potential nickname alert

Larky, Spark, Nark.

Latifa

Origin and meaning
Arab origin, meaning 'delicate'.
Queen Latifa is an American actress and singer, and
Latifa Echakhch is a French artist who has exhibited
her work at Tate Modern.
Potential nickname alert
Queen, Lattie, Tifa.

La Toya

Origin and meaning
Hebrew origin, meaning 'the good'.
La Toya Jackson is a sister of the late Michael Jackson,
and La Toya Woods is a beauty queen from Trinidad
and Tobago.
Potential nickname alert
Laté, Toyota.

Lavender

Origin and meaning
Latin origin, meaning 'purple'.
Lavender Brown is a fictional character in the *Harry
Potter* novels and films, and Lavender is also a
character in Roald Dahl's novel *Matilda*.
Potential nickname alert
Lav, Lavatory.

Loretta

Origin and meaning
Latin origin, a variant of 'Laura' meaning 'crowned
with laurel'.
Loretta Swit is an American actress famous for her
role in the long-running 1970s sitcom *M*A*S*H*.
Potential nickname alert
Lori, Retta.

Lourdes

Origin and meaning
French origin, referring to the town in southern
France where the Virgin Mary is believed by some to
have put in an appearance in the 19th century.
In 1996 Madonna named her first daughter Lourdes.
Potential nickname alert
Loads, Madonna.

Lowri

Origin and meaning
Latin origin, a variant of 'Laura' meaning 'crowned
with laurel'.
Lowri Turner is a British television presenter and
journalist, and Lowri Morgan is a Welsh language
television presenter.
Potential nickname alert
Low, Lolo.

Lucinda

Origin and meaning
Latin origin, meaning 'light'.
Lucinda Lambton is a British writer and television presenter, and Lucinda Jenney is an American actress who has appeared in films such as *Rain Man* and *The Hangover*.
Potential nickname alert
Lucy, Cindy, Lulu, Lucifer.

Lulu

Origin and meaning
Arab origin, meaning 'pearl'.
Lulu is a British pop singer who was briefly married to Bee Gee Maurice Gibb, and Lulu Simon is the daughter of singer-songwriter Paul Simon.
Potential nickname alert
Lou, ToiletToilet.

Madonna

Origin and meaning
Italian origin, meaning 'my lady'.
Originally used to refer to the Virgin Mary in Christian tradition, the name is now far more commonly connected to a successful American pop singer and actress.
Potential nickname alert
Maddie, Donna, Lady Madonna.

Marina

Origin and meaning
Latin origin, meaning 'of the god Mars'.
Marina is a fictional character played by Jenny
Seagrove in the 1983 British film *Local Hero*, and
Marina Hyde is a British journalist and author of the
book *Celebrity*.
Potential nickname alert
Rina, Marinara, Harbour.

Mercedes

Origin and meaning
Spanish origin, meaning 'mercies'.
Mercedes Fisher is a fictional character in the British
television soap opera *Hollyoaks*, and Mercedes Lackey
is an American author of fantasy novels.
Potential nickname alert
Merc, Mercy, Sadie, Mercedes Benz.

Miley

Origin and meaning
Hawaiian origin, meaning 'vine'.
Miley Cyrus is an American singer and actress famous
for her role as Miley Stewart in the Disney series
Hannah Montana.
Potential nickname alert
Smiley, Mail, Milly.

Mimi

Origin and meaning
Italian origin, a variant of 'Maria' meaning 'beloved'.
Mimi Smith raised her nephew John Lennon, and
Mimi Spencer is a journalist and author of the book
101 Things to Do Before You Diet.
Potential nickname alert
Mimsy, You You.

Moon Unit

Origin and meaning
American origin, meaning 'one that orbits the moon'.
The name was coined by musician Frank Zappa for
his daughter who was born during the late 1960s
when the US was gearing up for its first moon shots.
Potential nickname alert
Moonie, Moo, Mooner.

Morwenna

Origin and meaning
Celtic origin, meaning 'white seas'.
Morwenna Banks is a British comedy actress, and
Morwenna Ferrier is a British journalist.
Potential nickname alert
Mo, Wenna, Morweena.

Myleene

Origin and meaning
Greek origin, meaning 'dark skinned'.
Myleene Klass is a British singer, pianist, author, presenter and astronomer who also happens to look good in a bikini.
Potential nickname alert
Miles, Millie.

Myrtle

Origin and meaning
Greek origin, referring to a type of shrub.
Myrtle Kaloiokalani Wilcox was a Hawaiian princess, and Moaning Myrtle is a fictional ghost character from the *Harry Potter* books and films.
Potential nickname alert
Mertie, Turtle.

Nefertiti

Origin and meaning
Ancient Egyptian origin, meaning 'the beautiful one has arrived'.
Nefertiti was married to the Egyptian Pharaoh Akhenaten and is credited with her husband for moving Egypt away from polytheistic religion towards worshipping only one god, Aten.
Potential nickname alert
Nevertitty, Nefer, Titty.

Neytiri

Origin and meaning

English origin, created for a fictional character in the 2009 James Cameron film *Avatar*.
Neytiri is a Na'vi princess in the film, and is played by American actress Zoe Saldana.

Potential nickname alert

Tiri, Avatar.

Olive

Origin and meaning

Latin origin, referring to the olive fruit.
Olive Oyl is Popeye's girlfriend in many mid-20th-century cartoons, and Olive Rudge is the frumpy sister of Reg Varney in the British sitcom *On the Buses*.

Potential nickname alert

Oil, Ollie.

Oonagh

Origin and meaning

Gaelic origin, meaning 'lamb'.
Oonagh McDonald was a British politician in the 1970s and 1980s, and Oonagh Mullarkey is a fictional character who appears in Marvel Comics as a mad scientist.

Potential nickname alert

Oonie, Nag.

Ophelia

Origin and meaning
Greek origin, meaning 'help' or 'assistance'.
Ophelia is Hamlet's loony lover who drowned herself in Shakespeare's Danish play, and Ophelia Dahl is the daughter of novelist Roald Dahl.
Potential nickname alert
Phelia, Fifi, Ophie, Fee, Get Thee To A Nunnery.

Oprah

Origin and meaning
Hebrew origin, meaning 'fawn'.
Oprah Winfrey is famous for being an American talk show host and businesswoman who became the world's first black billionaire.
Potential nickname alert
Opie, Opera.

Pandora

Origin and meaning
Greek origin, meaning 'giver of all'.
Pandora Braithwaite is a fictional character in the book and television series *The Secret Diary of Adrian Mole*, and Pandora Colin is a British actress who has appeared in the film *Run Fatboy Run*.
Potential nickname alert
Panda, Dora, Box.

Paris

Origin and meaning
French origin, referring to the capital city of France.
Paris Hilton is an American heiress and celebrity, and
Paris Jackson is the daughter of the singer Michael
Jackson.
Potential nickname alert
Paz, Hilton.

Peaches

Origin and meaning
English origin, referring to the fruit.
Peaches Geldof is the daughter of Bob Geldof and
Paula Yates, and Peaches Browning was an American
actress who in 1926 married a middle-aged
millionaire on her 16th birthday.
Potential nickname alert
Nectarines, Apples, Beaches.

Penelope

Origin and meaning
Greek origin, meaning 'weaver'.
Lady Penelope is a fictional character in the 1960s
children's television series *Thunderbirds*, and Penelope
Keith is a British actress who played Margo
Leadbetter in the 1970s sitcom *The Good Life*.
Potential nickname alert
Pen, Penny, Pitstop.

Persephone

Origin and meaning
Greek origin, referring to the daughter of Zeus in
Greek mythology.
Persephone is a character in the film *The Matrix*, and
Persephone Books is a British publishing company.
Potential nickname alert
Percy, Phone, Phonie.

Petal

Origin and meaning
Greek origin, meaning 'leaf'.
Petal Blossom Rainbow is the daughter of celebrity
chef Jamie Oliver, and Petal the Dog starred as herself
in the 2008 American television programme *Weird,
True & Freaky – Animal Feats*.
Potential nickname alert
Pet, Flower, Pedal.

Pixie

Origin and meaning
Celtic origin, meaning 'little fairy'.
Pixie O'Harris was the aunt of Australian artist Rolf
Harris, and Pixie Geldof is the daughter of former
pop star Bob Geldof and Paula Yates.
Potential nickname alert
Pixel, Pixar, Pickaxe.

Poppy

Origin and meaning
English origin, referring to the red flower.
Poppy Honey is the daughter of celebrity chef Jamie
Oliver, and Poppy Z. Brite is an American novelist.
Potential nickname alert
Pop, Pops, Ploppy.

Porsche

Origin and meaning
Latin origin, a variant of 'Porcius', meaning 'pig'.
Porsche is a German brand of luxury sports car, and
Porsche Pendleton is an actress who appeared in the
1995 film *Revenge of the Calendar Girls*.
Potential nickname alert
911, Boxter, Posh, Portion.

Portia

Origin and meaning
Latin origin, a variant of 'Porcius', meaning 'pig'.
Portia is a character in the Shakespeare play *The
Merchant of Venice*, and Portia de Rossi is an Australian
actress who appeared in the television series *Ally
McBeal*.
Potential nickname alert
Porsche, Tia, Porker, Portion.

Priscilla

Origin and meaning
Latin origin, meaning 'old'.
Priscilla Presley is the former wife of singer Elvis Presley, and *Priscilla Queen of the Desert* is a stage musical adapted from the 1994 film *The Adventures of Priscilla, Queen of the Desert*.
Potential nickname alert
Cilla, Silly.

Prunella

Origin and meaning
Latin origin, meaning 'plum'.
Prunella Scales is a British actress famous for her role as Sybil Fawlty in the 1970s sitcom *Fawlty Towers*, and Prunella Gee is a British actress who starred in the 1983 film *Never Say Never Again*.
Potential nickname alert
Pru, Nella, Prude.

Queenie

Origin and meaning
English origin, meaning 'female monarch'.
Queenie Watts was a British sitcom actress, and Queenie is a character based on Elizabeth I played by Miranda Richardson in the sitcom *Blackadder II*.
Potential nickname alert
Queer, Weenie.

Renée

Origin and meaning

Latin origin, meaning 'reborn'.

Renée Zellweger is an American actress famous for starring in many films including *Bridget Jones's Diary* and *Miss Potter*.

Potential nickname alert

Ren, Nay, Rainy.

Rowena

Origin and meaning

German origin, meaning 'happy fame'.

Rowena King is a British actress who has appeared in films such as *The Bucket List* and *Proof of Life*.

Potential nickname alert

Row, Weena, Ribena.

Roxanne

Origin and meaning

Persian origin, meaning 'star'.

Roxanne is a song by British band The Police about a prostitute, and is also the title of a 1987 film retelling the classic story *Cyrano de Bergerac*, starring Steve Martin and Daryl Hannah.

Potential nickname alert

Roxy, Foxy.

Ruby

Origin and meaning
Latin origin, meaning 'red'.
Ruby Wax is an American comedienne, and *Ruby* is a 1992 film about Jack Ruby – the man who shot and killed Lee Harvey Oswald at a Dallas police station in 1963.
Potential nickname alert
Rubes, Booby.

Sabine

Origin and meaning
Latin origin, referring to an ancient Italian tribe.
Sabine Kehm is a German ghostwriter and spokesperson for racing driver Michael Schumacher.
Potential nickname alert
Sabi, Saab, Bean.

Sabrina

Origin and meaning
Celtic origin, referring to the river Severn.
Sabrina Duncan is one of the fictional detectives in the 1970s television series *Charlie's Angels*, and Sabrina is a character in the children's animation series *Pokémon*.
Potential nickname alert
Sab, Rina, Witch.

Saffron

Origin and meaning

Arab origin, referring to the spice.

Saffron ('Saffy') Monsoon is the fictional daughter of
Edina Monsoon in the BBC sitcom *Absolutely
Fabulous*, and Saffron Burrows is a British actress who
appeared in the American television series *Boston
Legal*.

Potential nickname alert

Saffy, Sweetie Darling, Saffy Darling.

Sapphire

Origin and meaning

Greek origin, meaning 'gemstone'.

Sapphire is a fictional character played by Joanna
Lumley in the late 1970s British television series
Sapphire & Steel.

Potential nickname alert

Saffy, Sappy.

Seraphina

Origin and meaning

Hebrew origin, meaning 'high ranking angel'.

Seraphina Affleck is the daughter of American actor
Ben Affleck and actress Jennifer Garner.

Potential nickname alert

Sera, Seri, Phina.

Shakira

Origin and meaning
Arab origin, meaning 'grateful'.
Shakira Caine is the wife of British actor Michael
Caine, and Shakira is a Columbian pop star and
philanthropist.
Potential nickname alert
Shack, Kira, Sharky.

Shoshana

Origin and meaning
Hebrew origin, meaning 'lily'.
Shoshana Bean is an American Broadway stage actress
and singer, and Shoshana Damari was a Yemeni
singer.
Potential nickname alert
Shush, Shana.

Sigourney

Origin and meaning
Scandinavian origin, meaning 'the conqueror'.
Sigourney Howard is a fictional character in *The
Great Gatsby* by F. Scott Fitzgerald, and Sigourney
Weaver (born Susan Alexandra) is an American actress
who renamed herself after that character.
Potential nickname alert
Siggy, Siggs.

Solange

Origin and meaning
Latin origin, meaning 'solemn'.
Solange Dimitrios is a fictional character in the 2006 film *Casino Royale*, and Solange Knowles is the sister of American singer Beyoncé.
Potential nickname alert
Solar, Angie.

Tiger Lily

Origin and meaning
English origin, meaning a type of lily flower.
Tiger Lily is a fictional character from *Peter Pan*, the first film directed by Woody Allen was called *What's Up, Tiger Lily?*, and Tiger Lily is the daughter of Michael Hutchence and Paula Yates.
Potential nickname alert
Tigger, Tiggy.

Thelma

Origin and meaning
Greek origin, meaning 'wish'.
Thelma Chambers is a fictional character in the BBC sitcom *Whatever Happened to the Likely Lads?*, and Thelma Dickinson is a fictional character in the 1991 film *Thelma & Louise*.
Potential nickname alert
Thel, Thelm.

Tinkerbell

Origin and meaning
Literary origin, created by British author J.M. Barrie as a fairy character for his play and novel *Peter and Wendy*, later to become known as *Peter Pan*.
Potential nickname alert
Tinker, Tinky, Stinker.

Ulrika

Origin and meaning
Scandinavian origin, meaning 'wealthy heiress'. Ulrika Jonsson is a Swedish former weather girl and television presenter, and Ulrika Barkland Larsson was a Swedish EU Ambassador.
Potential nickname alert
Ulrika-ka-ka-ka, Eureka.

Una

Origin and meaning
Latin origin, meaning 'one'. Una Stubbs is a British actress famous for her role in the 1963 film *Summer Holiday*, and Una is a fictional character in Edmund Spenser's poem *The Faerie Queene*.
Potential nickname alert
Ooney, One.

Valentina

Origin and meaning
Latin origin, meaning 'strong'.
Valentina Igoshina is a Russian classical pianist, and
Valentina Tereshkova is a Russian cosmonaut who
was the first woman in space.
Potential nickname alert
Vally, Tina, Val.

Venetia

Origin and meaning
Latin origin, meaning 'from Venice'.
Venetia Scott is a British stylist and photographer,
and Venetia Burney named the planet Pluto in 1930
when she was 11 years old.
Potential nickname alert
Veny, Nisha, Venice.

Venus

Origin and meaning
Latin origin, meaning 'beauty'.
Venus Williams is an American tennis champion,
Venus Terzo is a Canadian actress and Venus de Milo
is an ancient Greek statue.
Potential nickname alert
Venice, Penis.

Violet

Origin and meaning
Latin origin, meaning 'purplish colour'.
Violet Bonham Carter was the grandmother of actress
Helena Bonham Carter, and Violet Affleck is the
daughter of American actor Ben Affleck and actress
Jennifer Garner.
Potential nickname alert
Violent, Purple.

Whoopi

Origin and meaning
English origin, made famous by American actress
Whoopi Goldberg (real name Caryn Elaine Johnson)
who was inspired by the practical joke toy known as a
'whoopee cushion'.
Potential nickname alert
Poopi, Whoopsi.

Winifred

Origin and meaning
Welsh origin, meaning 'holy' or 'peace'.
St Winifred was a 7th-century Welsh nun, and there
is said to be a healing spring at the site where she died.
Winifred Robinson is a BBC radio presenter.
Potential nickname alert
Winnie, Fred, Winnet, Winnie the Pooh.

Xanthe

Origin and meaning

Greek origin, meaning 'yellow' or 'blonde'.
Xanthe Elbrick is a British actress who has appeared
in the BBC television series *Doctors*, and Xanthe Terra
is a region of the planet Mars.

Potential nickname alert

Xan.

Xena

Origin and meaning

Greek origin, meaning 'foreigner'.
Best known from the television show *Xena: Warrior
Princess* starring New Zealand actress Lucy Lawless.

Potential nickname alert

Princess, Xenie, Zen.

Xenia

Origin and meaning

Greek origin, meaning 'hospitality'.
Xenia Onatopp is a character in the 1995 film
GoldenEye, and Grand Duchess Xenia Alexandrovna
of Russia was the daughter of Czar Alexander III.

Potential nickname alert

Xenie, Zen, Enya.

Yael

Origin and meaning
Hebrew origin, meaning 'ibex'.
Yael Stone is an Australian actress, Yael Flexer is an Israeli-born choreographer, and Yael Naim is a French singer-songwriter.
Potential nickname alert
Yell, Yellow.

Yolanda

Origin and meaning
Greek origin, meaning 'violet'.
Yolanda Charles is a British bass guitarist and singer-songwriter, and Yolanda Adams is an American gospel singer.
Potential nickname alert
Yo-Yo, Lander, Yellow.

Zafira

Origin and meaning
Arabic origin, meaning 'successful'.
A Vauxhall Zafira is a seven-seater people carrier with a range of engine sizes from 1.6 to 2.2 litres, and Zafira Boateng is an actress who has appeared in the television shows *Doctor Who* and *Holby City*.
Potential nickname alert
Zaffy, Fiery, Za-Za.

Zola

Origin and meaning
African origin, meaning 'quiet'.
Zola Budd is a South African athlete who is famous for running barefoot, and Zola Taylor was an American singer who was part of the group *The Platters*.
Potential nickname alert
Zoe, Cola.

Zsa Zsa

Origin and meaning
Hungarian origin, a variant of 'Erzsébet', which is a village in Hungary.
Zsa Zsa Gabor was a Hungarian-American actress, and Zsa Zsa Carter is a fictional character in the British television soap opera *EastEnders*.
Potential nickname alert
Jar Jar Binks.

Unusual Names
for Boys or Girls

Abba

Origin and meaning
Hebrew word for 'father', also said to mean 'born on a Thursday'.
Abba is the name of a 1970s Swedish glam rock band, and Abba Sabre is a French actor who appeared in the 2002 film *Abouna*.
Potential nickname alert
Mamma Mia, Fernando, Chiquitita, Banana.

Abbey

Origin and meaning
Latin origin, meaning 'father', a variant of 'Abigail'.
Abbey Bartlet is the fictional First Lady of the United States in the American television series *The West Wing*.
Potential nickname alert
Abbs, Flabby, Shabby.

Ariel

Origin and meaning
Hebrew origin, meaning 'lion of God'.
Ariel Sharon is the former Prime Minister of Israel, Ariel Moore is a character in the 1984 film *Footloose*, and Ariel is the protagonist in the Disney feature animation *The Little Mermaid*.
Potential nickname alert
Air, Mermaid.

Chesney

Origin and meaning

French origin, meaning 'from Chesnay', a town in France.

Chesney Hawkes is a British pop star who had a number one hit with *The One and Only*, and Chesney Allen was a British music hall comedian who was part of a double act with Bud Flanagan.

Potential nickname alert

Chess, Chestnut.

Corey

Origin and meaning

Gaelic origin, meaning 'hollow in a hill'.

Corey Feldman is an American actor who starred in films such as *The Goonies* and *Stand By Me*.

Potential nickname alert

Cor, Hardcore, Whorey, Apple Core, Corky.

Dakota

Origin and meaning

Native American origin, meaning 'friend'.

Dakota Fanning is an American actress who starred in the 2005 film *War of the Worlds*, and Dakota Blue Richards is a British actress who starred in the 2007 film *The Golden Compass*.

Potential nickname alert

Kota, Cody, Dak.

Didi

Origin and meaning
Dual origins, coming from German (meaning
'warrior'), and Latin (meaning 'desire').
Didi Pickles is the mother of two of the baby
characters in the children's cartoon series *Rugrats*.
Potential nickname alert
Dee, Diddy.

Dorota

Origin and meaning
Greek origin, meaning 'gift from God', a variant of
'Dorothy'.
Dorota Gawron was Miss Poland in 2007, and Dorota
Maslowska is a Polish novelist and playwright.
Potential nickname alert
Dot, Dorothy, Doris.

Erin

Origin and meaning
Gaelic origin, meaning 'from Ireland'.
Erin Brockovich is an environmental campaigner
whose story was the subject of a feature film in 2000
starring Julia Roberts.
Potential nickname alert
Rin, Eric, Urine.

Evelyn

Origin and meaning

Mixed origin, coming from both Hebrew, meaning 'life', and French, meaning 'desired'.
The novelist Evelyn Waugh liked his name so much that he married another Evelyn.

Potential nickname alert

Lyn, Eve, Evel, Evel Knievel.

Flynn

Origin and meaning

Gaelic origin, meaning 'redhead'.
Flynn Adam is an American rap artist, and Dr. Flynn Saunders is a character in the Australian soap opera *Home and Away*.

Potential nickname alert

Fly, Flintstone, Flid.

Golden

Origin and meaning

English origin, meaning 'the colour of gold'.
An extremely rare name. Golden Diamondz is a Canadian singer and dancer.

Potential nickname alert

Goldie, Goldilocks.

Jordan

Origin and meaning
Aramaic origin, meaning 'one who descends'.
Jordan is a British former glamour model and full
time celebrity, and Jordan Baker is a fictional
character in F. Scott Fitzgerald's novel *The Great
Gatsby*.
Potential nickname alert
Jo, Jordie.

Kai

Origin and meaning
German origin, meaning 'safe harbour'.
Kai Rooney is the son of British footballer Wayne
Rooney and television presenter Coleen Rooney.
Potential nickname alert
Kaiser, Kak.

Keeley

Origin and meaning
Gaelic origin, meaning 'born from a slim person'.
Keeley Hawes is a British actress who starred in the
television series *Ashes to Ashes* and *Spooks*, and Keeley
Donovan is a BBC weather presenter.
Potential nickname alert
Keels, Kiwi, Kelly.

Leighton

Origin and meaning
English origin, meaning 'sheltered town'.
Leighton Buzzard is Bedfordshire town, and Leighton Meester is an American actress who has appeared in films such as *The Roommate* and television shows such as *House*.

Potential nickname alert
Lee, Latie.

London

Origin and meaning
Indo-European origin, possibly meaning 'boat river'.
London Fletcher is an American football player, and London May is an American drummer.

Potential nickname alert
Paris, Londie.

Oriel

Origin and meaning
Latin origin, meaning 'golden'.
Oriel Agranoff is a British child actor who voices the lead character in the animation series *Charlie and Lola*.

Potential nickname alert
Ori, Oreo.

Piper

Origin and meaning
English origin, meaning 'pipe player'.
Piper Laurie is an American actress who dated Ronald
Reagan in her youth, and Piper Pinwheeler is a
fictional character in the animated film *Robots*.
Potential nickname alert
Pipe, Pippa.

Pudsey

Origin and meaning
As a first name, Pudsey comes from the injured teddy
bear from the BBC's *Children in Need* appeal show,
although it has older roots as a surname dating from a
thousand years ago.
Pudsey is also a small Yorkshire town, meaning
'Pudoc's island or riverbank'.
Potential nickname alert
Bear, Teddy.

Rainbow

Origin and meaning
English origin with hippy overtones, meaning exactly
what it says.
Rainbow Francks is a Canadian actor who starred in
the television series *Stargate: Atlantis*.
Potential nickname alert
Rainy, Rain, Ray, Bow.

River

Origin and meaning
English origin, meaning 'river'.
River Phoenix was an American actor who played the role of the young Indiana in the film *Indiana Jones and the Last Crusade*.
Potential nickname alert
Riv, Stream, Drip, Puddle.

Robin

Origin and meaning
English origin, meaning 'bright' or 'shining'.
A variant of 'Robert', the name is associated in literature with the medieval outlaw Robin Hood, and more recently with the American actor Robin Williams.
Potential nickname alert
Rob, Robbie, Hood.

Sage

Origin and meaning
Latin origin, meaning 'wise'.
Sage Stallone is the son of the American actor Sylvester Stallone, and Sage Walker is an American science fiction author.
Potential nickname alert
Saggy, Stage.

Tatum

Origin and meaning
English origin, meaning 'tearful bringer of happiness'.
Tatum O'Neal is an American actress who won an
Oscar at the age of 10 and went on to date Michael
Jackson and to marry John McEnroe.
Potential nickname alert
Autumn, Tantrum.

Toyah

Origin and meaning
Hebrew origin, meaning 'good' (a variant of 'Tovah').
Toyah Willcox is a British actress and former punk
singer, and Toyah Battersby is a fictional character in
the British television soap opera *Coronation Street*.
Potential nickname alert
Toyota, Toy.

Whitney

Origin and meaning
English origin, meaning 'white water'.
Whitney Houston is an American singer, and
Whitney Willard Straight was an American-born
racing driver who also served as an RAF fighter pilot
in World War II.
Potential nickname alert
Witty, Houston, Nitwit.

Willow

Origin and meaning

English origin, meaning 'willow tree'.

Also known as the title of a fantasy film and a character from *Buffy the Vampire Slayer*. The actor Will Smith named his daughter Willow Camille Reign Smith.

Potential nickname alert

Willy, Wills.

Zowie

Origin and meaning

Greek origin, meaning 'life'.

A variant of 'Zoe', it was given to David Bowie's first child who later rejected it and called himself 'Duncan' instead.

Potential nickname alert

Zo, Wee.

Appendices

Top 10 Names for
Most Intelligent Boys
(2009)

1. Alexander

2. Adam

3. Christopher

4. Benjamin

5. Edward

6. Matthew

7. Daniel

8. James

9. Harry

10. William

Top 10 Names for
Most Intelligent Girls
(2009)

1. Elisabeth
2. Charlotte
3. Emma
4. Hannah
5. Rebecca
6. Abigail
7. Grace
8. Alice
9. Anna
10. Sophie

Top 10 Names for Most Popular Boys in the Classroom (2009)

1. Jack
2. Daniel
3. Charlie
4. Callum
5. Benjamin
6. Connor
7. Adam
8. Alfie
9. Christopher
10. James

Top 10 Names for Most Popular Girls in the Classroom (2009)

1. Emma
2. Charlotte
3. Hannah
4. Anna
5. Caitlin
6. Chelsea
7. Courtney
8. Holly
9. Brooke
10. Jessica

Top 10 Names for Baby Boys (2009)

1. Jack
2. Oliver
3. Charlie
4. Harry
5. Alfie
6. Thomas
7. Joshua
8. William
9. James
10. Daniel

Top 10 Names for Baby Girls
(2009)

1. Olivia
2. Ruby
3. Sophie
4. Chloe
5. Emily
6. Grace
7. Jessica
8. Lily
9. Amelia
10. Evie

www.crombiejardine.com